<u>NOT</u> THE OFFICIAL LAWYER'S HANDBOOK

NOT THE OFFICIAL LAWYER'S HANDBOOK

KEVIN P. WARD, ESQ.

A PLUME BOOK

NEW AMERICAN LIBRARY

NEW YORK AND SCARBOROUGH, ONTARIO

Copyright © 1984 by Kevin Patrick Ward
All rights reserved
Photographs by Ulli Geister and the Vegas Studios
Illustrations by Tracey Crowther

 PLUME TRADEMARK REG. U.S. PAT. OFF. AND FOREIGN COUNTRIES
REG. TRADEMARK—MARCA REGISTRADA
HECHO EN HARRISONBURG, VA., U.S.A.

SIGNET, SIGNET CLASSIC, MENTOR, PLUME, MERIDIAN and NAL BOOKS are published
in the United States by New American Library, 1633 Broadway, New York, New
York 10019, *in Canada* by
The New American Library of Canada Limited, 81 Mack Avenue,
Scarborough, Ontario M1L 1M8

Library of Congress Cataloging in Publication Data

Ward, Kevin P.
  Not the official lawyer's handbook.

  1. Law schools—United States—Anecdotes, facetiae,
satire, etc. 2. Law students—United States—
Anecdotes, facetiae, satire, etc. I. Title.
KF287.W28 1984   340'.07'1173   84-486
ISBN 0-452-25507-4

Designed by Barbara Huntley
First Printing, August, 1984
1 2 3 4 5 6 7 8 9
PRINTED IN THE UNITED STATES OF AMERICA

THIS BOOK IS DEDICATED
TO MY MOTHER,
MY BROTHERS,
AND DAD—WHO, WHEN
TOLD THAT I HAD BECOME
A LAWYER, MUTTERED,

"Pity. He
could have been
a writer."

CONTENTS

ACKNOWLEDGMENTS xiii

INTRODUCTION xv

SECTION I
WHEN I GROW UP I WANT TO BE A LAWYER 1

Filling Out Your Application 1

CHAPTER 1
THE LEGAL APTITUDE TEST
Do You Really Have What It Takes to Be a Lawyer? 3
You Be the Judge (A Self-Test) 3

SECTION II
ONE-L: The Rites (and Wrongs) of Passage 11

CHAPTER 2
PRETRIAL PREPARATION
Essential Study Tools for the Fledgling Legal Eagle 13

Study Groups: Threat or Menace? 13
Study Group Short-Form Analysis 16

CHAPTER 3
LEGAL LINGUISTICS FOR LAYMEN
The Long and Short of Becoming Cunning Linguist 19

How to Speak Legalese: A Foreign-Language Primer 19

Make It Brief: How to Brief Cases on Your Own Until the Bookstore Gets That Shipment of Canned Briefs 23
f u cn rd ths, u cn mk L. Rev. 27

CHAPTER 4
BEATING THE SEATING CHART
You Are Where You Seat 32

The Best Seats in the House 33
The Back-of-the-Bus Gang: A View from the Rear 36

CHAPTER 5
THE CLASSROOM AS COURTROOM
Making the Socratic Method Work for You 38
The Casebook Method 38

The Socratic Method: A Sordid Overview 39
Escaping from S/M: How to Pass with Class 41

CHAPTER 6
DIVERTISSEMENTS
Games to Keep You Awake in Class 46

Asshole Bingo 47
College Bowl 51
Football Pool 53
Beat the Clock 54
Bogus Briefs: The Glickfeld Reporter 54

ix

CHAPTER 7
MAKING THE GRADE
The GPA as a Religious Quest   57

Pre-Launch Preparation   58
Taking the Test: IRAC and Beyond   58

CHAPTER 8
MURDERER'S ROW
A Guide to Your First-Year Courses   64

Criminal Law and Procedure   64
Contracts   66
Constitutional Law   69
Civil Procedure   70
Torts   71
Property   73

SECTION III
YOUR WORLD AND WELCOME TO IT:
From the Collective Unconscious to the Collected Unconscionables to the Collection of Unmentionables   77

CHAPTER 9
THE COLLECTIVE UNCONSCIOUS
What Every Law Student Must Know   79

Significant Cases and Concepts   79
Smooth Judges and Why We Like Them   81
Neanderthal Laws (Statutes and Rulings) That Are Still on the Books   83

CHAPTER 10
THE PRE-INDICTMENT LINEUP
Law School's Cast of Characters   87

The Students: A Bestiary   88
The Professor: Law School's Most Perfectly Evolved Subspecies   104

CHAPTER 11
LAW SCHOOL SOCIAL LIFE
Nothin' from Nothin' Leaves Nothin'   110

Where the Action (Such as It Is) Is   110
How to Library: A Frisky Guide from the Mezzanine to the Back Stacks and Back   113

CHAPTER 12
LAW REVIEW
How to Become The Crème de la Crème   119

Law Review Editors   119
Making Law Review: The Necessary Legal Pedigree   119
Moot Court: The Unkindest Cut of All   122

SECTION IV
THE TRIALS OF JOB
From Interview to Offer in Three Easy Kung-Fu Moves   125

CHAPTER 13
OFFENSIVE INTERVIEWING
"I am in the top 10% of my class, I'm on Law Review, I love your firm, and this gun is loaded."   127

The Interview   129
Interviewing the Interviewer   131

Body Language: How to Read
Your Interviewers Like a
(Tawdry) Book   132
How to Handle Rejection   136

CHAPTER 14
THE BIG-FIRM SUMMER
CLERK'S EXPERIENCE
Midsummer Knight's
Dream   139

Identifying the Proper Firm:
Separating the Blue Chip from
the Buffalo Chip   139
Handling Yourself with
Aplomb   140
Office Politics: Anything Worth
Doing Is Worth Doing avec
Savoir Faire   141

SECTION V
BREEZING THE BAR
Bambi Meets Godzilla   143

CHAPTER 15
BAR WARS
A Look at the Bar Examiner's
Empire   145

An Inspirational Message from the
Publishers   145
Equal Opportunity Response from
the Writer   145
The Sorrow and the Pity: A
Historical Overview of the Bar
Exam   146
Your Alternatives: None   148

CHAPTER 16
BAR TREK
Preparing to Boldly Go Where
No Man Has Gone Before (and
Survive)   149

Become a Bar Review Rep and
Save $800   149
Choosing a Bar Review
Course   150

CHAPTER 17
IN THE BELLY OF THE BEAST
A Personal (Horrifying) Account
of the Exam   152
Suzy-Q's Diary   152

CHAPTER 18
ADDING INSULT TO INJURY
How the Examiners Decide Your
Fate   162

The Bar Exam: The Inside
Story   163

SECTION VI
"A" IS FOR ATTORNEY
Talking, Thinking, and
Billing Like a Lawyer   169

CHAPTER 19
LAW FIRMSMANSHIP
From Peon to Partner in Five Easy
Pieces   171

Tote That Barge: How to Carry a
Partner's Briefcase   172
Midnight Express: The Importance
of Being Earnest   173
The Brooks Brothers
Manifesto   173
The Kowtow Catalogue   174
Make No Mistake About It   175

CHAPTER 20
POWER WORDS
A Glossary of Big-Firm
Metaphors and Buzzwords for
Heavy Hitters   176

CHAPTER 21
LEGALTHINK:
State of Innocence v. State of
 Siege 185

Do You Think Like a Lawyer
 Now? 185

ACKNOWLEDGMENTS

First the good news: there is still a haven where a would-be writer can ply his trade without being arrested—the Café Figaro in Greenwich Village. Bernie Bodo and the gang can always be counted on to provide the proper blend of bohemian atmosphere and industrial quantities of cappuccino required to create dubious literary achievements like this one. Now the bad news: I would be remiss if I did not mention certain people who aided me in this project, and since I still owe most of them money, some of them have threatened me with physical bodily harm if they did not receive their due. Since I strongly suspect that they aren't kidding, I would like to take this opportunity to express my undying devotion and offer a year's supply of choice chicken parts to the following co-conspirators: Susan Byrne, red-haired vixen, whose undaunted research unearthed legal esoterica that still eluded the author after weeks of digging, such as the names of the present Supreme Court justices; Andrea Stein, genius, who helped to get the proposal for this book accepted; Bob Egan of King Literary Agencies, who, through hardheaded negotiation, was able to coerce NAL to put the second royalty check in his name (by the way, if you know of his whereabouts, I'd very much appreciate hearing about it); Louise Betts, for her tireless devotion to two of America's enduring institutions—the written word and the King of Rock 'n' Roll; Ann Waterfall, a most talented, charming, and diplomatic editrix ("Now, Kevin, I would be the last person to use the phrase 'incredibly bad taste' in referring to that last paragraph, but isn't there some way you could just change a little word here and there, just to, um, tighten it up?"); Alison Karlsson, fair-haired saint and all-round business manager, who transformed reams of unintelligible hieroglyphics of deranged ranting to reams of beautifully typed, perfectly spelled deranged ranting; William (Murph the Surf) Murphy, Jr., who accidentally sent an appellate brief in the manila envelope with his cameo guest chapter (as it was impossible to tell one work of humorous fiction from the other, I included his brief as another chapter—what a bonus!); Lisa Ronis, whose expertise in psychotic behavior proved invaluable in writing this book, in that she knew when to leave me alone; and especially

Tracey Crowther, artist, who took time out from her demanding pursuits of slam-dancing and the quest for the perfect Margarita to create the mini chefs d'oeuvre that appear throughout this book.

Now, as you can imagine, a book of this scope and magnitude is not possible without a substantial amount of research and plagiarism, and I would like to use this space to thank all of the terrific people from whom I "borrowed" instructive passages. They shall, unfortunately, have to remain nameless, since the new Copyright Act has made everyone so touchy about other people's borrowing their stuff, even when it is done in the spirit of fun.

I would also like to thank the following institutions: Harvard Law School; Yale Law School; Hastings College of Law; LSDAS; LSAT; ETS; New York University Law School; Boalt Hall (University of California at Berkeley); Cornell Law School; The New York Committee of Bar Examiners; the American Bar Association; the U.S. National Asshole Bingo Rules Committee; the Committee of Bar Examiners of the State of California; the NYU Placement Office; the Hastings College of Law Placement Office; Pillsbury; Madison & Sutro; Cravath, Swaine & Moore; Dillingham and Murphy; the Chris Ward Foundation for the Arts; BAR/BRI; Josephson BRC; Stanley Kaplan Bar Review Course; and *American Lawyer*. Some of the foregoing schools, firms, and companies were a big help in aiding my research on the book, and some are just thrown in to give it some class.

Ulli Geister and the Vegas Studios are responsible for the photographs, so any lawsuits should be directed at them. The models, whose camera-ease comes from posing for numerous police lineups, are members or friends of the "Not-Ready-for-Prime-Numbers" troupe: Uncle John (the only professional in the group), Wendy Ettinger, Mark O'Donnell, Sunny Bates, Fred Newman, Pete Christy, Lisa Vaamonde, Tony DeRose, Greg and Chris Maya, Ingrid Rosselini, Thomaso, Gerda Ronis, Scott Campbell, Louise Betts, Lisa Ronis, Alison Karlsson, Andrea Stein, Michael Hunold, Robin Pasch, Suzy Byrne, Larry Spagnola, Joan Leydon, Larry Cummings, Hannah Wall, Tracey Crowther, Monique Martin, Diane Sinnot, and other luminaries.

INTRODUCTION

King Henry VI, in an expansive mood after being elected Chairman of the Entertainment Committee for the third year in a row, enthusiastically outlined his ideas for new and fun activities for the fall season. "The first thing we do," he cheerfully proclaimed, "let's kill all the lawyers." His dinner companions chided him for his bad sentence structure, but he pointed out that it was the Middle Ages and everybody talked like that.

Even if we forgive him his English (it *was* the Middle Ages), and his choice of kidney pie as an entree (he *was* English), there is no reason to let him get away with such a churlish remark, even if it was uttered in an outburst of élan. Let's admit it. The world needs lawyers.

A world without lawyers would be as chaotic and incomprehensible as those "E-Z Read" New York Subway maps where you start off going crosstown and you end up in downtown Sri Lanka. There would be mayhem—and to make matters worse, nobody would be making any money off the mayhem. Citizens of all so-called "civilized" countries would be squabbling with each other, saying nasty things, filing for bankruptcy, and generally making the world an unpleasant place in which to live.

But, thank God, there are plenty of attorneys to do all of the squabbling, name-calling, and filing for bankruptcy, while our plucky paisans sip Pernod and dash off bits of blank verse in the charming bistros of their choice. Lawyers define, test, confirm, and force reevaluation of the fundamental societal rights of individuals, frequently while the individuals in question are lounging around the house in terry-cloth bathrobes. It is the lawyers and judges who take these ineffable, abstract phantasms and transform them into comprehensible black-letter law (except for corporate lawyers, who do the exact opposite).

Lawyers are an integral part of the natural order of things. If God hadn't meant us to have lawyers he would not have created corporations and divorce. (Now, there are probably some purists out there who are saying, "God didn't create corporations and divorce—Man did!" But they are just splitting hairs and looking for a chance to get into a pointless religious argument, and this book is above such petty ad hoc behavior.)

So the only question left for an intelligent individual (other than "Why did I shell out several clams for this book when I could have gotten the Triple Burrito Special at Manuel's Taco Palace?") becomes "How do I become one of the chosen few? How can I transform my meaningless, dilettantish existence of champagne, caviar, and movie premiers into 80 hours a week of stimulating, relevant footnote research in a gargantuan antitrust case that will be settled as soon as the Republicans are reelected?" In short, "How do I become a lawyer?"

Our intelligent individual has posed a valid query, rife with hidden hopes and fears, and it deserves a sincere, cogent, well-considered answer. Not surprisingly, as with most seemingly complicated and many-faceted dilemmas, the answer to this imposing question is elegant in its simplicity:

Buy this book.

If you are bright, literate, and contemplating law school (although the former qualities tend to rule out this last), or are already in attendance, your decision to buy this book is the wisest one you will make in your legal career (and it is the only one that may possibly absolve the idiocy of your decision to become a lawyer).

Not the Official Lawyer's Handbook will enable you to glide through law school with the ease of Cary Grant charming his way through a cocktail party. Having perused *Not the Official Lawyer's Handbook*, you will dress appropriately, speak legalese like a veteran trial attorney, exhibit a precocious understanding of significant cases and judges, and know exactly how to finesse your way onto Law Review and into the mega-firm of your dreams. Effortlessly. At this point, it would be unfair not to warn you that attempting law school without this guide is as rash and ultimately fruitless as trying to figure out what the hell everyone in *La Traviata* is doing without program notes.

And if you are already a lawyer, admit it—law school was the most intense, challenging, exhilarating, and memorable experience of your life. And all those books and movies by laymen haven't done it justice— you have to have lived through it, sort of like having fought on the beaches at Guadalcanal or the "Charo" Christmas Special at Vegas. You need something that will "bring it back alive": the adrenaline rush when you stood up to recite your first brief in class; your professor's first respectful acknowledgment of you in front of your peers —"Wrong, Bozo Breath." The first complaint you wrote using form books—where you found out you were suing yourself (I get misty-eyed just thinking about it).

But are there any books that can do this without having to resort to personal threats? In fact, are there any fun books for lawyers to read other than *Commercial Paper* and *Secured Transactions*—my personal favorites—that are written just for them? No! Nothing! *Nada!* None of the above! Until now.

Not the Official Lawyer's Handbook is a book whose time has come. For years, disrespectful pundits have been gratuitously mocking, insulting, and belittling law students, lawyers and the law, just for the fun of it. It's high time somebody got paid to do it.

K. P. W.
(somewhere near the Supreme Court of the United States)
December 1983

SECTION I
WHEN I GROW UP
I WANT TO BE A
LAWYER

☐ FILLING OUT YOUR APPLICATION

**Application for Admission to Harvard Law School – Part 2
September 1984**

Full Name ___BEGG___ ___ANN___ ___FAWN___
(Last) (First) (Middle)

Please present yourself and your qualifications as you wish in a brief statement below. You may wish to explain or to draw the attention of the Committee to a particular part of your record or application. You may also wish the Committee to consider achievements and qualities not otherwise revealed by the application. Additionally, this form may be used to complete answers to questions on the application or to make any other comments which you believe are relevant. We ask that you confine your remarks to the space below, or no more than one additional page.

I wish to become an integral part of Harvard Law School's vital contribution to the legal community, specifically in the area of mergers and acquisitions.

Effective

**Application for Admission to Harvard Law School – Part 2
September 1984**

Full Name ___Byrne___ ___'bABE'___ ___bUrN___
(Last) (First) (Middle)

Please present yourself and your qualifications as you wish in a brief statement below. You may wish to explain or to draw the attention of the Committee to a particular part of your record or application. You may also wish the Committee to consider achievements and qualities not otherwise revealed by the application. Additionally, this form may be used to complete answers to questions on the application or to make any other comments which you believe are relevant. We ask that you confine your remarks to the space below, or no more than one additional page.

When the revolution comes And you bourgeois ~~pigs~~ dogs Are strung up by your bloated thumbs, I want to be the bloody sword of vengeance Enforcing the Will of the Proletariat!

Not-So-Effective

CHAPTER 1
THE LEGAL APTITUDE TEST
Do You Really Have What It Takes to Be a Lawyer?

Sure, you look good in a Brooks Brothers suit. You were voted "most argumentative" by your classmates, and you successfully defended yourself in that drunk-driving case, where your Honda wound up in the birdbath in the middle of your neighbor's lawn.

But do you have that certain *je ne sais rien* quality that distinguishes a good lawyer from an oversized gecko lizard? The following questions, taken from actual hypotheticals, test your analytical ability and psychopathic tendencies. Read the questions *closely*. All the facts are important. Score yourself using the answer key at the end of the chapter. No peeking.

☐ **YOU BE THE JUDGE (A Self-Test)**

PSYCHOLOGICAL PROFILE

1. A civilian without lawyers is like
   a) a JAP without credit cards.
   b) a Margarita without salt.
   c) a state trooper without sunglasses.
   d) a Hare Krishna without black high-top basketball shoes.

2. Your life's dream is
   a) sailing around the world, across the seven seas.
   b) climbing Everest, feeling the wind in your hair.
   c) hang-gliding serenely among the seagulls in Hawaii.
   d) smoking two packs of cigarettes a day, drinking 14 cups of coffee, and holing up with 72 *Federal Reporters* which you must have memorized by Monday.

3. Who do you feel has contributed most to society and makes the world a better place?
   a) Mother Theresa
   b) Martin Luther King
   c) Gandhi
   d) Roy Cohn

4. A lawyer is most like a
   a) brain surgeon.
   b) Broadway conductor.

c) electrician.
   d) platypus.
5. What activity would you undertake if you had only one week left to live?
   a) I would start a wild, debauched orgy and die of overindulgence.
   b) I would take the first flight to Tibet and seek quick enlightenment.
   c) I would travel the streets of America, giving all my money to the poor.
   d) I would sue as many people as I could, given the time constraints.
6. You view law as
   a) a seamless web where wise men search, like Demosthenes, for elusive truth.
   b) a fast way of making huge bucks.
   c) a cute concept, but not as well thought out as *Hogan's Heroes*.
   d) an aphrodisiac.
7. A lawyer's role in society is
   a) defending the oppressed.
   b) offending the depressed.
   c) goaltending the distressed.
   d) distending the prepressed.
   e) behind the wheel of a new Ferrari.

ANALYTICAL ABILITY

8. Which of the following guarantees a citizen the best protection from criminal elements?
   a) the 1st Amendment
   b) the 4th Amendment
   c) the 5th Amendment
   d) a .50-caliber machine gun

9. You are riding in a cab when it careens around a corner and strikes an old lady.
   You
   a) administer first aid and call for help.
   b) offer to sue the cabbie on behalf of the old lady.
   c) offer to defend the cabbie if the old lady sues.
   d) sue the cabbie for whiplash, and then sue the old lady for causing you emotional distress when you saw her get hit.

10. Rodney hired Vangoe to paint a personal portrait of Rodney "to Rodney's personal satisfaction." Vangoe spent one month painting, then presented the portrait to Rodney, who refused to pay. Vangoe sues for the money.
    Which of the following arguments will most likely succeed in Rodney's defense?
    a) Three pedestrians said it looked like an ad for gefiltefish, with Rodney playing the gefiltefish.
    b) Vangoe used pastels, instead of the Day-Glo paint on black velvet that Rodney had specified.
    c) Vangoe deliberately portrayed Rodney wearing a red dress. Vangoe *knows* it makes Rodney look pale.
    d) Rodney, in the picture, looks exactly like Barbara Streisand. Come to think of it, *all* of Vangoe's paintings look exactly like Barbara Streisand.

e) Rodney died yesterday.

11. Marcia purchased a bottle of skin lightener and applied it as directed, and her breasts grew to the size of Rhode Island. She sued the store, the manufacturer, and a local TV personality who referred to her on the air as *"an oversized flotation device."*

    Marcia will most likely prevail on which of the following theories?
    a) A consumer can *reasonably expect* to use a personal cosmetic without having to get air clearance from the FAA ten minutes later.
    b) Being called "an oversized flotation device" would not *reasonably* be construed as being paid a big compliment by someone, even in Queens.
    c) The instructions on the cosmetic did not even *mention* Rhode Island.
    d) A Ms. Andrea Schwartz from Great Neck purchased a bottle of the same skin lightener from the same store soon after Marcia and is now employed as a high-altitude reconnaissance dirigible.

12. In a "Retreat" self-defense jurisdiction, a victim must retreat before using deadly force on an attacker *unless*
    a) the attacker is wearing Sergio Valente jeans.
    b) the victim has said, "Tag, tag, no hit-backs!"
    c) the attacker is a vocal fan of John Denver.
    d) the victim is in the shower, and the attacker is intentionally flushing the toilet so that the victim alternately freezes and boils.

13. Which is the most effective technique of determining the sentence of a convicted felon?
    a) counsel deliberation
    b) jury deliberation
    c) judge deliberation
    d) three-card monte.

14. Marty is arrested for stabbing Howie 17 times in the back in a local bar. Which of the following is the *best* defense?
    a) Marty acted in the *heat of passion* because Howie was going to name all 22 counties of New Jersey for the 18th time.
    b) Marty *mistook* Howie for the Electrolux salesman who had accidentally vacuumed Marty's four pet parakeets into oblivion at a free home demonstration.
    c) Marty was *unaware*: "I was just cleaning my knife when this guy comes running into the bar and runs into it backwards 17 times...honest!"
    d) Marty made a *mistake of law*; he was not *aware* that stabbing someone was illegal in this jurisdiction, although he had a hunch it might be.

15. When addressing the jury, a lawyer should
    a) try to remain fully clothed, if possible.
    b) look each juror directly in the eye, except for that fat lady in

row three who has her false eyelashes stuck together.
c) avoid waving $50 bills in front of the jurors prior to deliberation (this makes the judge jealous).
d) always sign off with: "You've been a wonderful audience—just great!—I love ya, get outta here!"

16. Louise is eating dinner at a New Wave restaurant. The music is so loud it knocks out her sense of taste, and she spends 10 minutes dipping potato chips unerringly into the can of Sterno which is heating the bean curd dip. She suffers indigestion and sues the restaurant, the Sterno manufacturer, and the Leather Nuns (the band).

Louise will most likely prevail on which of the following theories?
a) The Sterno was not listed on the menu, and the waiter didn't mention it as a special, so it was an *unforeseeable* appetizer.
b) The Sterno's flavor was *identical* to that of the bean curd dip, although it was a little less spicey, so Louise acted *reasonably* in eating the whole can.
c) Louise was charged $3.25 (plus tax) for eating the Sterno.
d) The deafening volume of the Leather Nuns turned the hair of one of her companions dark puce and turned her other companion into a homosexual.

17. Capital punishment should apply to which of the following groups?
a) people who use the word "ergo" at cocktail parties
b) individuals who purchase oil paintings of those kids with big eyes—you know the ones
c) EST graduates
d) the Bee Gees

CASE ANALYSIS

18. Homicide: Issues of Actual Causation—Who Is To Blame?

At the rainbow Room, for their 20th anniversary, Mabel lovingly orders Lester a piña colada with a fresh pineapple wedge, a brightly colored straw, a maraschino cherry, and a healthy dose of slow-acting rat poison that is fatal within two days. As they leave the restaurant, an Albanian terrorist group grabs Lester's black velveteen oversized necktie and throws him from the 63rd floor, where he is shot by an Afghan marksman.

As he sails by the 60th floor, an Iroquois warrior impales him with a poison arrow. He is garroted by the cord of the RCA Building flagpole at the 54th floor. From the 53rd floor to the 46th floor, he is filmed for a cameo in a Martin Scorsese movie. At the 43rd floor, he is hit by a low-flying helicopter piloted by a disgruntled Vietnam veteran. Spinning end over end, he slams into a gargoyle on St. Patrick's Cathedral across the street and is sandblasted for the next eight floors by Mel's Master

Blasters, Inc., which rebounds him across the street, where he is struck unceremoniously by a cleaver thrown by an enraged sushi chef, who is distraught over unfair treatment of the Japanese under the Marshall Plan.

As Lester falls limply past the 29th floor, a waiter, who has just been fired by the Rainbow Room for commiting indecent acts with a floral arrangement, puts a hand grenade in Lester's pocket. At the 25th floor he is machine-gunned by a parachutist, and as he falls past the 12th floor, he is hit in the chest by a killer boomerang thrown by a crazed aborigine. He finally falls into a tank trap dug by the Daughters of the American Revolution.

Q. Who is guilty of Lester's murder, based on the above facts? Respond in essay form.

SELF-SCORING

Score your answers accordingly, then see how your total rates in the "Self-Rating" section. This will determine whether you should become a lawyer or continue your successful bookie operation.

1. a) 2
   b) 2
   c) 4
   d) 6
2. a) 0
   b) 0
   c) 0
   d) 6

If (d) doesn't turn you on, drop out and take up surfing. Seriously.

3. a) 0
   b) 0
   c) 3
   d) 6

Gandhi is worth a few points because he was a lawyer at one time even though he copped out later.

4. a) 6
   b) 3
   c) 2
   d) 6
5. a) 2
   b) 1
   c) 0
   d) 6
6. a) Are you kidding?
   b) 4
   c) 2
   d) 6
7. a) What, are you nuts?
   b) 3
   c) 2
   d) 3.7
   e) 6
8. a) 1
   b) 2
   c) 3
   d) 6

A lawyer can be theoretical, but he's got to be practical, too.

9. a) 0
   b) 3
   c) 4
   d) 6
10. a) 3
    b) 3
    c) 3.2
    d) 4
    e) 6

This tests your ability to tell gefiltefish, Day-Glo paint, and Barbara Streisand apart, essential skills to a lawyer, especially in litigation.

11. a) 6
    b) 2.7
    c) 1
    d) 4

12. a) 4
    b) 4
    c) 3* (or 5 if there is a John Denver Christmas Special on at the time)

13. a) 1
    b) 2
    c) 3
    d) 6

14. a) 6
    b) 4
    c) 1
    d) 1

15. a) 2
    b) 2.7
    c) 1
    d) 6

16. a) 3.4
    b) 3.2
    c) 2
    d) 7

The nuances of *foreseeability* are explored here, with emphasis on the similarity in taste between tofu and Sterno—a characteristic that will undoubtably affect tort law in the post-holistic era.

17. a) 3
    b) 3.2
    c) 4
    d) 3.7
    e) If you wrote in "none of the above" or left it blank, you are either too soft or lack the proper zeal to be an attorney. If you wrote in anything else, give yourself 10 points. If you wrote "lawyers," read no further. Use this book for a paperweight at your mailroom job.

18. A: No one. Lester did not die. He did, however, get a severe case of heartburn from the escargots at the Rainbow Room, for which he is suing. (Give yourself 40 points if you got this one right.)

SELF-RATING

5–30 points: Hopeless Idealist
Listen—the world *needs* idealistic philosopher-carpenters, but the law doesn't. Do *not* go to law school; you would just spend most of your time telling other students your revelations on how pointless, unethical, and unfulfilling law is. They will not consider you a voice in the wilderness; they will consider you a pain in the ass.

30–55 points: Public Interest Lawyer
You are under some delusion that law is the means for generating beneficial social change for the downtrodden in society.

Don't worry. This condition is normal for someone who has not yet attended law school, and will certainly disappear by your second-year interview. Remember: "Law doesn't generate small change for the masses; it generates big bucks for the partners."

55–75 points: Sharpshooter.
Most red-hot lawyers come from this category. You are a sweetheart, but

you completely understand and embrace your role as an attorney, which is to say you love your mom, and have dinner with her every Friday, but you would not hesitate to sue her ass off if you were ever assigned the case by a partner at your firm.

Some people will say that lawyers are like mercenaries, but that's an unfair comparison—there are some things a mercenary will refuse to do.

75–110 points: Law Dog

The world is your oyster. Law school has *thousands* of books with fine print, and *endless* rows of carrels where you can be left alone to study. When you're on Law Review there will be millions of cities to check, so nobody will catch you peeking at your "Second Security Deed of Trust" treatise hidden between the covers of a *Playboy* magazine. They won't suspect a thing.

The 200-person law firm you will join will have showers and changing rooms, so you will never have to leave the library, ever! It's almost sinful, we know, but you were born to be a Law Dog. Live it up!

110+ points: Zen Master/Legal Eagle

Don't waste any more time. Get in touch with the Harvard Law School faculty and they'll sign you up immediately. You are much too dangerous to be left on the streets.

Getting Into Harvard Law School Made Easy

SECTION II
ONE-L: THE RITES (AND WRONGS) OF PASSAGE

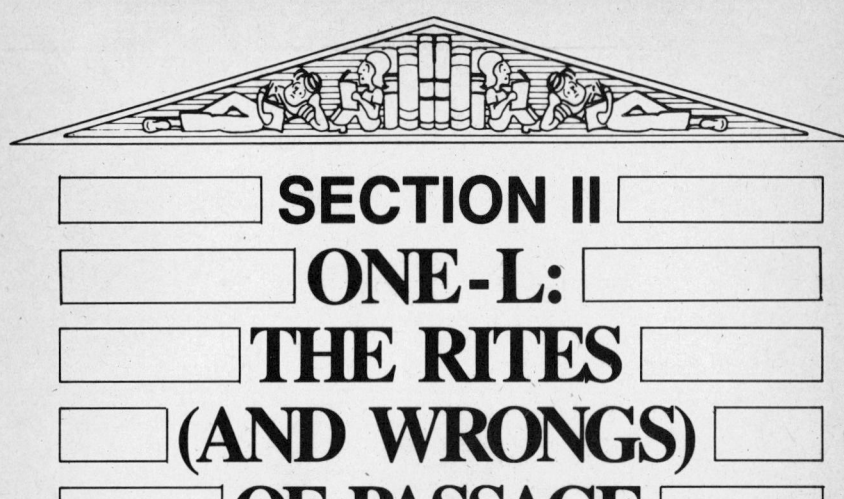

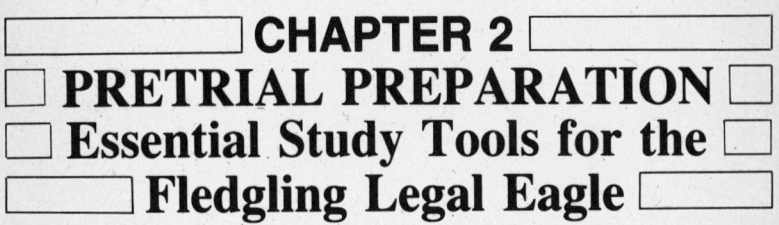

CHAPTER 2
PRETRIAL PREPARATION
Essential Study Tools for the Fledgling Legal Eagle

Dante, when asked by an admirer what, exactly, *The Inferno* referred to, replied crisply, "Law school, you silly-willy, especially levels 5 and 7. Remember, I met Socrates. Do I have to spell it out for you?" Chastened, the fan slunk away, tail between his legs—and so he should have, because law school is the single most famous rite of passage in history, as well as the most arduous, combining elements of the *Odyssey*, the labors of Hercules, the myth of Sisyphus, and the Voyages of Laverne and Shirley into a gauntlet of mythic proportions, where only the truly worthy survive.

We intend to reverse that trend, giving you all the secret passages, safe harbors, and magic amulets you'll need to not only survive, but thrive, emerging victorious from the journey with a $50,000-a-year first-year associateship—trust us. Let's start with the tools of the trade.

☐ STUDY GROUPS: THREAT OR MENACE?

Study groups are a sociological gathering phenomenon endemic to arsonists, Green Berets, and law students. The main motivating force behind them is, of course, a common interest in humanity and the desire to help others. But, believe it or not, there are other reasons. Before we get into those, though, let's try this little pop quiz. Circle the correct statement:

A. Law students share a common bond in their search for knowledge. Through incessant sharing of ideas, vigorous interchange of opinion, and a communal synthesis of information, they strive for a collective excellence that will benefit all of society some day.

B. A law student is in it for himself. He would not give artificial res-

☐ 13

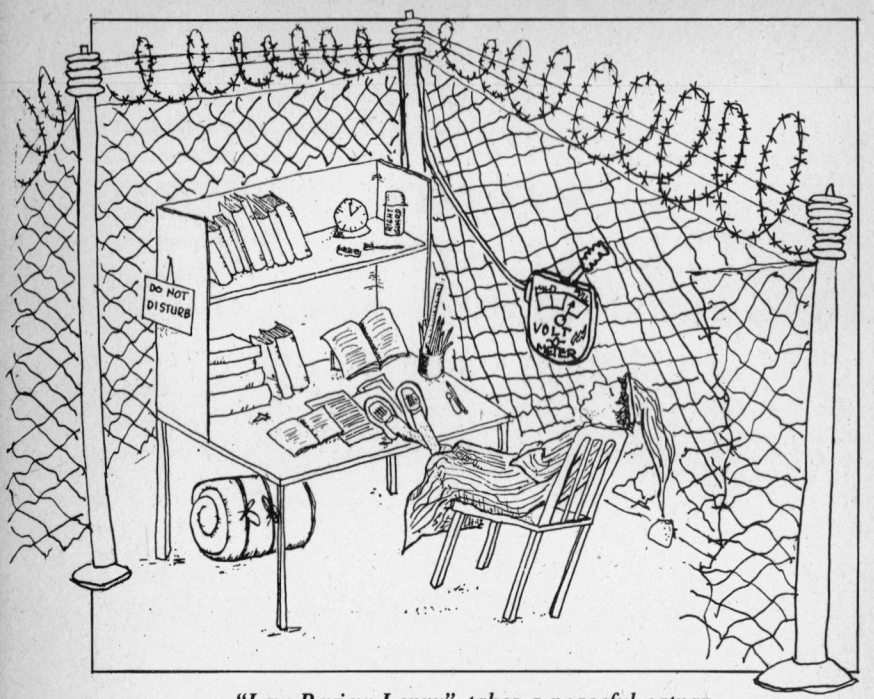

"Law Review Lenny" takes a peaceful catnap, confident that his Electro-Fry electric fence, with built-in Voltometer, will toast intruding classmates.

piration to a stricken classmate unless he was sure the victim was going to help the curve if revived. Law students make Harvard premeds (who sabatoge each other's experiments regularly) look like philanthropists.

If you circled A, your naiveté is charming; it would be of immense help in some people-related profession. But this is law school, sport. Nobody helps anybody else in any way unless he is positive that he will benefit more in the long run (and short run, too).

Which brings us back to study groups.

Early on, it became apparent to law school professors that students were not sharing their notes or ideas. Professors noticed the fold-out fiberglass walls that each student erected around his books before class, the pup tents popping up in the library covering the carrels, and the triple-bolt locks students were installing on their lockers. And the fact was, students were taking up a lot of the professors' time asking questions they could have answered themselves if they would only discuss them with other students. So, knowing that each student's sole goal was to get better grades than the competition, the professors started a rumor that by banding into study groups and sharing notes and outlines, "study groupers" could leave the competition in the dust. Then the profs systematically gave higher grades to kids who were in study groups to give credibility to the rumor. And voilà—study groups became a law school institution, and profs got to hit the golf courses right after class instead of being stuck in their offices, answering obvious questions.

So you're going to join a study group. It's as inevitable as buying textbooks. There are advantages—if you join a good one, and stay together through second year, you will be able to cut your attendance to 25% (i.e., each of you becomes responsible for a turn taking notes while the other three skip class).

This is not to say, however, that you should go rushing in blindly, accepting the first gilt-edged invitation that comes your way.

Give it some thought. Your study group experience can shape your whole law school career. For example, if one member of your study group is so obnoxious that you are driven to bludgeon him to death with his 50-pound outline, then you won't be allowed to graduate, and your legal future would be ruined by a silly little mercy killing (although you would probably be acquitted—judges remember how obnoxious their study group partners were). So to be on the safe side, follow these guidelines:

Choosing Your Study Group

As this will be one of the most important decisions you will make in law school (other than the decision to strangle your Property professor, discussed later), you owe it to yourself to do some research so that you make the right choices for study group mates. But the choice is not an easy one.

The horns of your dilemma are twofold (isn't it interesting how the horns of a dilemma *always* seem to be twofold?).

Horn 1: You want to get your group started immediately so you can catch up with the already overwhelming caseload.

Horn 2: It's only the beginning of the year. No one has broken from the pack, so you can't tell the aces from the jokers yet. But there's no time to wait. What to do?

Fortunately, the Bureau of Study Group Statistics has derived a relatively simple formula for determining whether a hot prospect belongs in your group or conversely, whether you belong in that swift group you are coveting. The BSGS also has a more comprehensive logarithmic formula, but refused to share it with us, in characteristic "we got ours, you find your own" study group fashion. So here is the short-form test.

Simply fill in the following for yourself and then repeat the process for each prospective groupmate.

☐ STUDY GROUP SHORT-FORM ANALYSIS

LSAT Score:	50	49	48	47	46	45	44	42	40	38
points:	10	9	8	7	6	5	4	3	2	1

Undergrad GPA:	4.0	3.9	3.8	3.7	3.6	3.5	3.4	3.3	3.2	3.1	3.0
points:	20	18	16	14	12	10	8	6	4	2	1

Personality:
Saint — 10
Sweetheart — 9
Vaguely tolerable — 8
Barely tolerable — 7
Nebbish — 6
Turk — 5
Hun — 4
Philistine — 3
Assassin — 2
Premed — 1

Typing ability:
Nonexistent — 0
Two-finger — 3
80 wpm — 5

Own study aids?
Yes — 0
No — 2

Classroom attendance:
100% — 5
95% — 4
90% — 3
80% — 2
70% — 1
14% — 0

Quality of notes:
Great — 10
Good — 15
Mediocre — 0
(Score a 0 if notes are illegible, regardless of quality.)

Available Saturday & Sunday nights:
Yes — 5
No — −5

(This is a critical question. Anyone who thinks he or she will have the time to go out dining and dancing on weekends during law school is seriously self-delusional.)

Connections:
Related to senior partner in a big firm — 3
Related to senior partner in a small firm — 2
Related to professor — 1

(Such connections are worth a few peripheral points because they may get you an interview or be able to pass along tips on the upcoming test.)

Now add up the points accompanying your attributes, then try to get into a group where each of the other students has a higher cumulative score than yours. You can then breathe easy and be as helpful as you want, confident in the knowledge that you are exploiting them. (Actually, law students' general paranoia results in an amazing parity between members in study groups. Anyone who doesn't measure up will be immediately—and brutally—dropped.)

How Successful Will Your Study Group Be?

Unless your goal is to put yourself through law school by playing poker with your group, there is only one question you should have in mind: "If I put up with these three grindaholics for a whole year, what will I get out of it?"

Fortunately for you, the all-purpose Study Group Formula, in its infinite and versatile wisdom, also flawlessly predicts the eventual success of members of a particular study group based on the group's averaged score.

Here is the breakdown:

	Aces	Face Cards	Jokers
Average LSAT	10	5	2
GPA	20	10	4
Personality	10	5	1
Typing	5	3	0
Study aids	2	2	2
Attendance	5	4	1
Notes	10	5	0
Weekends	5	5	1
Connections	3	1	0

TYPICAL STUDY GROUP: Aces

Don't underestimate the value of study groups. By the end of the year, all students will be sufficiently skillful to study on their own, and most groups will break up. But some will stay together and will benefit mutually. The members of one group at a noted law school all joined Law Review together, became district court clerks, and are now district court judges in the same circuit. They still convene regularly to compare decisions! The members of another group in the same school were so evenly matched, their studying technique so similar, that they got identical grades in all of their classes. Unfortunately, the grade was F, so they flunked out simultaneously. They remained together, however, and are now known as the Marx Brothers.

The moral of the story is—join a study group. There *is* strength in numbers.

TYPICAL STUDY GROUP: Jokers

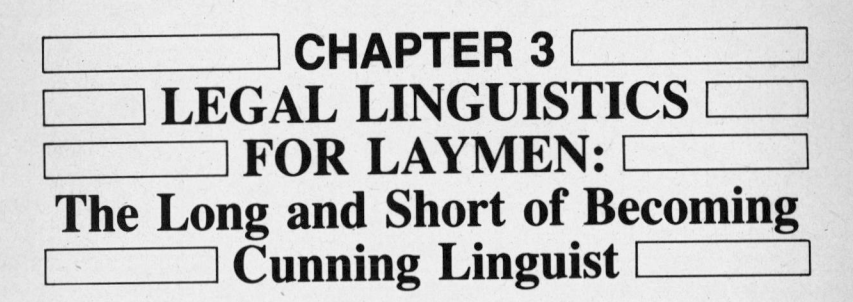

CHAPTER 3
LEGAL LINGUISTICS FOR LAYMEN:
The Long and Short of Becoming Cunning Linguist

☐ HOW TO SPEAK LEGALESE: A Foreign-Language Primer

The most critical skill you will acquire in law school is the ability to turn clear, concise English sentences into a convoluted mass of arcane jargon, circumlocutory syntax, and anisotropic sentence structure—style guaranteed to render your every phrase incomprehensible to all but your legal brethren. It is imperative that you learn this as soon as possible, or else you won't be able to impress your friends, your professors will be convinced that you haven't learned anything, and your parents will wonder what you've been doing with the tuition money. *Note*: It is as important to be able to read legalese for 18 hours (or 240 pages, whichever comes first) as it is to be able to write it. So get to it. You've got to learn sometime. And no skimming. Each *word* is important.

Directions: For best results, read this primer out loud, quickly, with clear and forceful tone. In no time, you'll be tripping "heretofore" off your tongue with the ease of a 50-year attorney.

LESSON 1:
DICK ASKS JANE FOR A DATE English Version

DICK: Would you like to go out on a date?
JANE: Yes.

Ho, hum. This is so clear, your four-year-old brother could figure out what is going on here. But watch what happens when we add a few elementary buzz words and inflate it with hyperventilating syntax—voilà! Verbal landfill! Just compare:

DICK ASKS JANE FOR A DATE Legalese Version

DICK: **1.(a)** Definitions: Whereas the Party of the First Part, designated hereinafter as "Offeror," or "Hot

20 □ ONE-L: THE RITES (AND WRONGS) OF PASSAGE

Hello, Francine?

Don't "Hello" me you jerk. You know perfectly well that you made an implied oral contract for a date last night which I reasonably relied upon to my detriment and which you materially breached by your extreme and outrageous conduct, proximately causing me to suffer a prima facie case of emotional distress and ...

LEGALESE MADE EASY Lesson #4: The Phone Call

Stud," desires to initiate contact, orally, physically, or by any other means recognized under present technology or that which becomes available hereafter, with the Party of the Second Part, hereinafter referred to as "Offeree," "Promisee," or "That Incredible Blonde with the Set of Major League Yabboes." For the purpose or purposes, individually, collectively, or in installments, of communicating in English, Pig Latin, or any other universally recognized medium (including but not limited to French, Spanish, Rude Animal Sounds, and Sign Language), the substance, in whole or in part of the offer contained in 1(c),

it being understood by both parties that such offer is to be construed in accordance with, and subject to, the definitions and stipulations enumerated in this section, if any, and

(b) The Offeror (or Offeror's agent acting within the scope of his employment) certifies that he has full legal contractual capacity and possesses sufficient age, discretion and mental capacity (notwithstanding a brief period wherein Offeror ingested two tablets of mescaline and took the Walt Disney "Pirates of the Caribbean" amusement ride 147 times in a row, vigorously maintaining that he was Francesco da

Silva, Terror Rogue of the High Seas, and attempted to impale other patrons with a two-foot-long apricot dried fruit roll) to make the following offer, but asserts that if Offeree or any third party seeks to enforce said offer, it is hereby understood that such offer is voidable due to certain discrepancies in the Offeror's IQ, to the tune of lack thereof.

(c) Offeror, as defined in Section 1 (a) and (b) for just and sufficient consideration, without giving rise to any liability thereby, hereby, whereby, or hair pie, makes the following offer, which may be accepted by Offeree but is expressly made inalienable, free from anticipation or assignment, attachment, or pledge by any of Offeree's successors in interest, including but not limited to heirs, assigns, devisees, or interested third parties, except for Offeree's redheaded roommate, with the quick wit, charming smile, and alarmingly streamlined chassis that would give heart palpitations to a sedated orangutan, said acceptance being subject to the same equitable and legal defenses enumerated in 1(a) and (b) and any other defenses available under law or equity or any other systems of thought now known to Mankind, or which may become known in the future.

(d) At the time of communication of said offer (or within a reasonable time thereafter not to exceed three months) Offeree will be empowered to accept such offer, which will be referred to hereinafter, whereinafter, hereunder, thereunder, hither, and thither as an offer and/or request for a "DATE" which will be construed hereafter as an activity, or series of activities, undertaken jointly and severally, for the mutual enjoyment of one or both parties thereunder, including but not limited to:

☐ Eating rancid Twinkies in the law school cafeteria;
☐ Squeezing the lemon wedges by the coffee/tea urn in the cafeteria to make lemonade;
☐ Studying directly across from each other at the library ("study date");
☐ Or any number of other similar wacky activities;

the understood purpose of said activity to initiate, promulgate, engender, and/or promote a general perception on the part of Offeree of increased intimacy, real or construed, with the Offeror, resulting in further activities including but not limited to a little nooky, heavy petting, the activity referred to as "The Horizontal Mamba," "The Dance with No Steps," "Dancing in the Dark," or any combination thereof.

JANE: **1.** Offeree, having been apprised of the aforementioned offer for a "DATE" as defined in Sections 1(a), (b), and (c), hereby avers as follows (clauses will be discussed seriatum): Offeror will be referred to hereinafter as Promisor, Party of the First Part, Nerd, Tool and/or Sniveling Worm, such terms to be employed interchangeably.

2. (a) There Can Be No Meeting of the Minds—Offeror Has No Mind to Meet. The Party of the Second Part hereby contests the contractual capacity of the Party of the First Part, directing the court to take judicial notice of the former's lack thereof, as evidenced by the supporting affidavits (which are incorporated by reference hereby as if set forth below), certifying that Offeror (or "Pressed Ham")

1. "is a prime example of an evolutionary stopgap measure" (Appendix A);
2. "is playing with one frontal lobe tied behind his back" (Appendix B);
3. "is playing with a deck with no facecards" (Appendix C);
4. "gives new meaning to the term 'lunchmeat'" (Appendix D).

And to the extent that such offer is void or voidable by Offeror (hereafter "Spongehead"), it is not binding on Offeree, except to the extent that it gives rise to or preserves Offeree's contractual rights and remedies upon acceptance of such offer, including but not limited to an acceptance modifying terms or made expressly conditional upon the addition of new and different terms, analogous to Uniform Commercial Code Sections 2-207, *et seq.*, including "Buyer's Remedies for Disposal of Rotting, Nonconforming Fungible Goods."

(b) Conditional Acceptance.
Without accepting in the legal sense, Offeree hereby purports to maybe, possibly, potentially accept to a limited extent those portions of the offer listed below which are determined by the court to consist a valid and enforceable offer only insofar as such enumerated portions are not partially or totally inconsistent with any or all of the clauses contained herein, including this one, such acceptance being hereby made expressly conditional on the following terms, it being understood by both parties, particularly Offeror (or "Spam Brain"), that the failure of *any* part of *any* or *each* or *all* or *every* or *some* or *one teensy eensy weensy bit* of *each* and *every* condition, individually, collectively, or otherwise, will constitute a major breach of such condition, rendering the contemplated acceptance (and subsequent laughably remote agreement) NULL AND VOID as though it never existed, such nullity applying retroactively to the date of the offer, or more accurately, the Offeror's seventh birthday, whichever came first, and any disagreement as to which came first will be determined by binding arbitration between petitioner and respondent, with the result being the same: no tickee, no washee, Buffalo Breath.

(c) Condition Defined: Minimum Requirements for Date.
The condition which must be satisfied completely prior to any duty, right, or obligation arising respecting the contemplation of a conceivable acceptance of the "offer" is nondivisible in that it must be performed all at once without a lot of whining and bellyaching, and is composed of the following elements:

Offeror (or "Fungus Face") must certify under penalty of perjury in the presence of at least two witnesses, one of whom must be awake and the other of whom must be a deputized notary public, that the "DATE" he is contemplating involves some activity which, viewed under circumstances most favorable to the Offeree, would be construed by a person possessing reasonable intelligence, reasonable taste, and a reasonable capacity for excruciating boredom, to constitute an undertaking which has the potential to generate at least as much interest or amusement as Offeree could experience individually by engaging in self-abuse and/or lapsing into a mild coma for the entire evening, such decision to be made by an uninterested and fully clothed magistrate; which is subject at all times to modification or rejection by Offeree or any successors in interest, including my redheaded roommate, who asserts that she would rather "nosedive for matzoballs" than contemplate the potential of the offer, which she views with the same enthusiasm as a 12-hour bout with whooping cough or, in the alternative, a root canal, which means that the offeree hereunder is primarily and exclusively responsible for the answer communicated hereunder:

"NO"

ANALYSIS

For obvious reasons, out of the 40,000 law students who graduate annually, only 14 have gone out on dates. By the time they finish with the asking and answering, it is time to get back to studying, and if either one is trying to be coy, instead of straightforward (as Dick and Jane are), it can take up to three days. As a result, most students settle for reading pornographic cases or fantasizing. They fantasize about everything from getting an A in Torts to becoming an associate at Coudert Brothers.

But even if you do not wish to plunge into this frantic dating scene, if you are thinking about law school, or are a first-year student, try to get a grasp of the enemic flow of legalese. You will know you're close when you become aware that any statement or question is potentially infinite—limited only by your imagination and stamina. And for those of you who are already associates or partners and feel you have mastered legalese, there is a way to test your skill—close your eyes, point your finger, and bring it down on the contract on your desk; then pick the closest comma and insert a clause of infinite duration. It should be as effortless as breathing.

☐ MAKE IT BRIEF: How to Brief Cases on Your Own until the Bookstore Gets that Shipment of Canned Briefs

Next to choosing study aids and buying amphetamines, the most important survival skill that the first-year student must master is the fine art of briefing cases. In every class, a student, when called upon, must present a short synopsis of a case (hopefully, the one being discussed), organized according to the

24 □ ONE-L: THE RITES (AND WRONGS) OF PASSAGE

KNOW YOUR BRIEFS
Lesson #26: Basic Brief Recognition

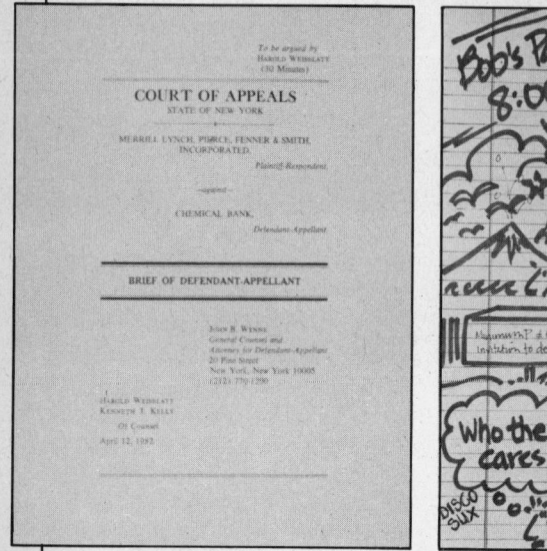

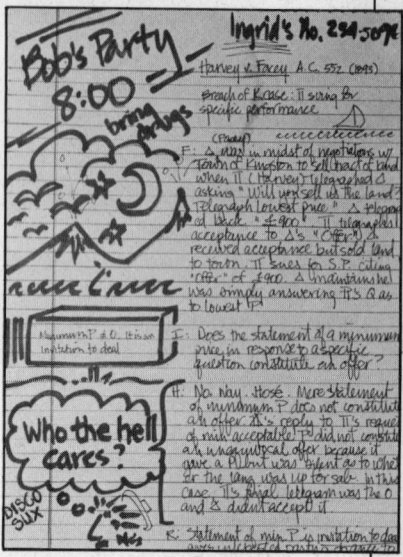

Appellate

Classroom

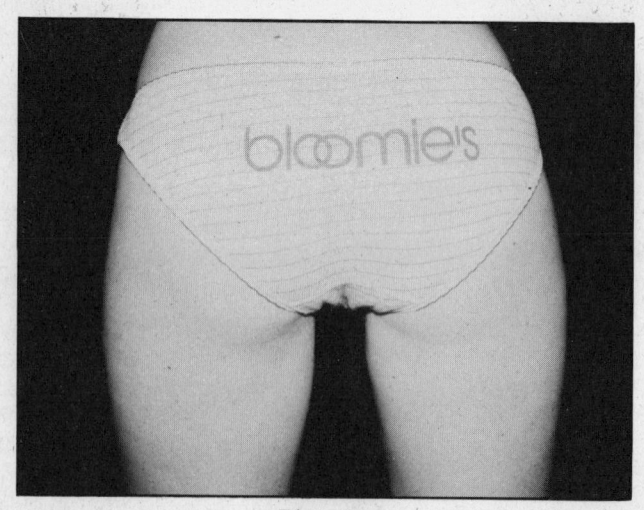

Bloomies

professor's specifications. This is called a "brief".*

Most professors prefer some variation of the Facts/Issue/Holding/Rationale pattern, but each has his own preference. One professor at Yale Law School required his students to begin each brief with a Henny Youngman joke, followed by a quick rendition of "I Feel Pretty" from *West Side Story*.

Brief-writing accomplishes two major goals in a professor's educational scheme. First, by forcing students to condense a 20-page case into one page, the prof increases the odds that they will have left something out, which makes it easier for him to humiliate them in class; and second, by making students responsible for at least four cases a day per class, the prof guarantees that they will be at home with bloodshot eyes and dog-eared textbooks at 1:00 a.m., so he won't have to worry about bumping into any of them at the Underground Disco (and being bored to death by having to make legal small talk).

There are four general approaches to briefing cases, each with its unique advantages (familiarity with the cases) and disadvantages (lack of social life). But don't worry;

---

*Do not confuse the in-class "brief" with the "brief" that a practicing attorney writes when appealing a case. With an in-class brief, the object is to distill a longwinded court opinion, full of muddled facts, issues, and irrelevancies, into a concise synopsis in which the facts, issues, and conclusions are succinctly stated. With an appellate brief, the object is to do the exact opposite.

you won't have to pick the style you feel most comfortable with—it will pick you.

The four most common approaches to briefing cases can be categorized by degrees of compulsive tendencies:

1. There is the *New-Book* method, in which you read each case, underlining Facts, Issue, Holding, Rationale, and Dictum (if it's a Con law case or a good judge), then go back over it, condensing the facts, etc., into one page. Go over it again, just to make sure. Finish at 4:00 a.m. Start briefs for next class.

2. There is the less rigorous *Used-Book* technique, which entails reading already-underlined Facts, Issue, Holding, Rationale, etc., condensing as you go along. Avoid unmarked areas like the plague. Finish at 9:00 p.m. Go to a movie.

3. The *Canned-Brief* approach is elegant in its simplicity: Read canned brief. Underline if you're in the mood. Finish at 2:00 p.m. Go to the beach, then restaurant, then movie, then nightclub.

4. *Book-Briefing* takes practice. For the ultrasmooth who have learned how to wing it in class straight from the book, without committing anything to paper, this is the way to go. This style usually doesn't emerge until second year, by which time the students are bored with preparing briefs and are no longer afraid of profs, so they're willing to chance it.

The following brief is an example of the most popular format required by professors.

PARTIES

Mrs. Ferrington (P) President Reagan (D)

ACTION

Plaintiff seeks to enforce permanent injunction in federal court preventing Defendant from starting nuclear war, based on implied contract between P and D.

FACTS

Mrs. "Babs" Ferrington (P) corresponded with President "Bonzo" Reagan (D), offering him 14 pounds of her famous Alice B. Toklas brownies in return for a promise from D that he would not start a nuclear war and annihilate civilization "without giving it some serious thought." She received a written reply from the offeree (D) which in essence said, "Let's see the brownies first." She sent the brownies and received notification that D had "eaten the whole batch and really gotten off on them." Assuming that D had accepted the contract, P began work on building the swimming pool she had always wanted. However, three weeks later, she received word that D, after losing in Scrabble 13 times in a row to a bellhop with a Russian surname, had declared nuclear war on Russia. P, citing her implied-in-fact contract, sues in federal court seeking to enjoin the nuclear attack at least until the contractors finish the deep end of her pool. D maintains that the brownies, while "totally awesome," did not constitute sufficient consideration to create a contract binding him to forbear from nuclear war. D further maintains that nuclear war "is not a woman's business."

ISSUE

Do 14 pounds of "totally awesome" brownies constitute sufficient consideration for forbearance of a nuclear attack?

HOLDING

Yes. The courts will not test the adequacy of consideration.

RATIONALE

It is well settled that consideration is not tested for adequacy. Traditionally, a "mere peppercorn" is enough to bind parties to a contract—so imagine what Babs' brownies, which paste you to the ceiling for 13 hours, can do.

This established rule of law has been adhered to faithfully in recent holdings: *Katz* v. *Three Chinese Waiters and That Fat Guy in the Corner*, 131 U.S. 261; *Kwik Kleaners* v. *One Brooks Brothers Blazer and an*

Unnamed Meatball, 217 U.S. 451; and most recently, *Mrs. O'Hallahan v. The 125th Street Salsa Rhythm Devils*, where the court found that homemade cherry cobbler constituted sufficient consideration for forbearance of an all-night bongo concert.

So there's the format. Simply read your brief in a loud convincing tone, ignoring the lentil soup stains on the rationale, and you're in business.

A caveat

Professors warn, every year, that it is suicidal to read directly from canned briefs in class. They are right. This is because *they* read directly from canned briefs in class, and will recognize the syntax immediately. If you are so foolhardy as to try it anyway, they will then humiliate you by asking you esoterica that's not in the canned briefs, such as "On what page in the casebook does this case begin?" or "Could you please read me paragraph 4 verbatim?" Of course, if you're fast enough on your feet, have a casebook, and are sitting next to a helpful buddy, maybe you'll emerge unscathed. But it's edgework. And the footing is precarious.

☐ *f u cn rd ths, u cn mk L. Rev.*

In law every single word is important. If you doubt this, just try the following exercise:

"Counselor, I find your client _____." Now insert one of the following three words: "guilty," "innocent," "bananas." See what a difference one little word makes?

Unfortunately, this means that you must take very comprehensive and accurate notes in class (or have other sources—see "Study Groups," above), which will require either developing 80 wpm penmanship or a system of substantially abbreviating recurrent words. Later in this chapter we provide tips on speedwriting,* but more important, we list all of the standard abbreviations you will need to enable you to take notes and still have time to look up from your pad occasionally to flutter your eyelashes at the prof. If you already know shorthand, so much the better. Not only will notetaking be a breeze, but no one will be able to copy off your notes—an essential competitive edge.

Abbreviations will mean different things depending upon the context (i.e., PC means "proximate cause" in Torts, "probable cause" in Criminal Procedure, and "puke city" in Modesto, California). Similarly, abbreviations (abb) can mean different things to different people (d/p). Following are choice excerpts from the notebooks of a Back of the Bus Gang Member (B/B) and a Law Review Editor (Wimp).

As you will see, some of these abbreviations can have dramatically different meanings for each student, while others appear to have no meaning at all, to anybody.

*No we don't. This isn't a damn kindergarten book. Do you want us to take your tests for you too?

28 □ ONE-L: THE RITES (AND WRONGS) OF PASSAGE

Abbreviation	Law Review Editor	Back of The Bus Gang
CB	casebook	canned briefs
P or π	plaintiff	punk, also cool guy
D or △	defendant	Drag Queen (close friend)
JN	jurisdiction	Jurassic nerd
SM	subject matter	sadomasochism
SMJN	subject matter jurisdiction	Jurassic nerd who's into S and M
F?	federal question	fox in question (the blonde in row 6)
Ct	court	cocktail
S Ct	state court	Sin City (Las Vegas)
F Ct	federal court	Fat City (sittin' pretty)
R↑	remove (from S to F Ct)	Redskins won
R↓	remand (from F Ct to S Ct)	Redskins lost
C/A	cause of action (claim for relief)	colossal asshole

CRIMINAL LAW

MPC	model penal code	medium-priced cocktail
GJ	grand jury	Greek, Jimmy the
A/B	assault and battery	Asshole Bingo
Hom	homicide	homo
Rd	reckless, depraved heart	Rodney Dangerfield
Burg	burglary	burgers (applied to all sandwiches)
LU	pre-indictment lineup	let's undress (note sent to paramour in class)
PV	plain view	to play Vegas (i.e., "The last time I played Vegas, it was 90 in the shade"); also, Puerto Vallarta
HP	hot pursuit	heavy petting
HS	hearsay	hot stud
W	witness	wimp

TORTS

Att N	attractive nuisance	good-looking tease
Neg	negligence	negligee
f?	question of fact (for jury)	well, does she or doesn't she?
f	reasonably foreseeable	you bet.
unf	unforeseeable	unfortunately, not a chance.
A	assault	Alpo
ED	intentional infliction of emotional distress (a parasitic cause of action)	Ed McMahon (same concept)
IP	inattentive peril	initial pass for the day (the result of inattentive peril)
Sl	slander	sleazebag (roommate)

CONTRACTS

K	contract	Kaluah
Quasi-K	quasi-contract (quantum merit)	any cocktail containing Kaluah
O	offer	the big O
Oee	offeree	the one who had the big O.
Or	offerer	the one responsible for the big O (can be the same person, unlike regular contracts)
2P	two-party contract	second pass of the week; things are getting tense
3PB	third-party	third pass blues—the inevitable professorial tongue-lashing that follows your third pass of the week
Cr B	creditor beneficiary	crab bait (ugly student/Law Review Wimp)
Br	breach	brewskis
Sub P	substantial performance	sub-par brewskis (slightly warm)

PROPERTY

Abbreviation	Law Review Editor	Back of The Bus Gang
BFP	bona fide purchaser	born on a farm in Peoria (moron)
Cov RL	covenant running with the land.	cover for me—I'm really loaded
D/	decedent (testator who died)	drunk/passed out
CL	common law	clueless
EP	easement by prescription	Elvis Presley, the King of Rock 'n' Roll
AP	adverse possession	anticipated punt (see "CL")
RAP	rule against perpetuities	rent a parachute (see CL, AP, supra)

Now see if you've got the swing of it. Try to interpret the following notes, first employing the Law Review dictionary, then the Back-of-the-Bus Lexicon. You'll see what we mean by different interpretations.

1. D guilty of first-degree A in S Ct based on criminal R/D acts.
2. Nabbed after 30 min high-speed HP = G. Neg.
3. D seeks R ↑ to F Ct.
4. Denied. R ↓ —S Ct GJ indictment stands. No reas. grounds for R ↑ .
5. Side issue: F? JN is impossible—crim.

LAW REVIEW INTERPRETATION

This is a synopsis of a Criminal Law/Civil Procedure case:

Defendant was found guilty of First Degree Assault in state court. Intent could be inferred from his actions, which were criminally reckless and depraved. Police caught him after 30 minutes of high-speed hot pursuit, which adds another count of gross (criminal) negligence. D seeks to remove to federal court. The motion is considered, then denied, and the case is remanded. The state court grand jury indictment, which he contested, is valid. No reason to remove the case. Side issue: D's attempt to claim Federal Question jurisdiction is impossible, since this is not a civil action.

BACK OF THE BUS GANG INTERPRETATION

This is a note passed from "Swifty" to his pal Matty, detailing the road trip he and his roommate took to Nevada last weekend:

Donny was a grade-A asshole in Vegas, based on his criminally bad

Rodney Dangerfield impersonations. Plus, I caught him engaged in a half-hour, high-speed petting session with a girl in a negligee—my little sister. In addition, this bozo bets heavy on the Redskins, maintaining he will be in Fat City when they win. Of course, the Skins lose. In Vegas, when Jimmy the Greek says a team will lose, they lose. That's all there is to it. You'd have to be crazy to bet on them. I rest my case—he was a complete spam brain.

P.S. There is no *way* that blond fox is going out with that wimp—it would be a *crime*!

CHAPTER 4
BEATING THE SEATING CHART
You Are Where You Seat

Kublai Khan was the first to notice the significance of seating charts, or more particularly, an individual's choice of location within the chart. He mused, "Warriors in front lines are very fierce, good fighters, but warriors in back rows tend to survive better, by a fifty-to-one ratio. Most interesting." And we would be foolish not to heed his observations, because, as George Santayana warned, "Those who do not learn from History are condemned to repeat it, or at best, get a D+.

So with all of those wise words ringing bilingually in your ears, let's examine one of the tautologies of law school: *You are where you seat.*

While some professors demand that students sit alphabetically, most

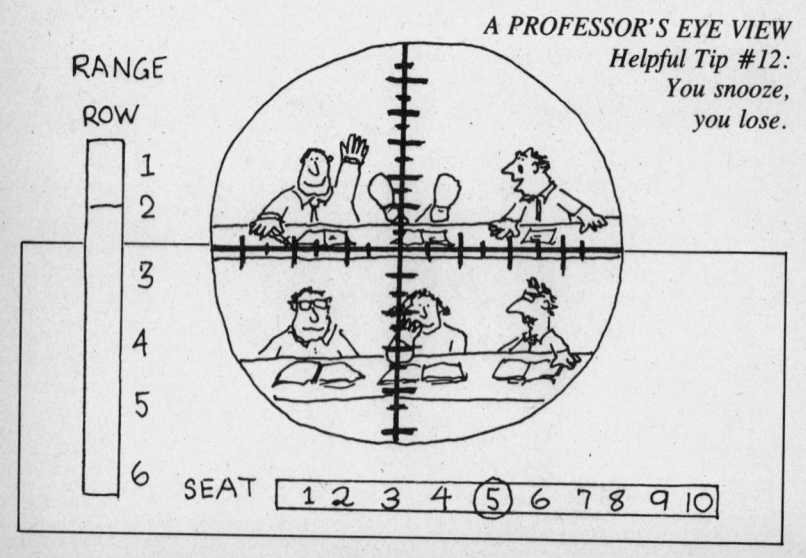

A PROFESSOR'S EYE VIEW
Helpful Tip #12:
You snooze,
you lose.

32

use a seating chart. This allows them to make it through the entire year without ever having to learn their students' names. There is usually a grace period of a week or so, during which you can try out different seats in the class. But you will have to make a decision: One day when you get to class, the chart will be passed around, you will sign your name, and your location will be locked in concrete for the rest of the year.

Do not underestimate the gravity of this decision. Depending on your final choice, you could spend your time in class surrounded by friends who will pass you their briefs and whisper answers when you're trapped, or by malevolent ferrets who cover their notes with both hands whenever you turn your head. You could be trading naughty notes with the cutest students in the class, or you could be breathing through an air purifier to avoid the study-sweat odor of the Law Review–bound weasel to your left.

☐ THE BEST SEATS IN THE HOUSE

Reserving the best seats in the house, seating-chart-wise, is an involved process. Of course, you should follow your instincts, but *only* after applying the following criteria:

The Strike Zone
Since professors rely on the students to do all of the teaching (see the next chapter), they tend to hit for average, which is to say they call on students who are sitting in certain areas that have proved to be red-hot hotbeds. This is how the strike zone looks to a prof:

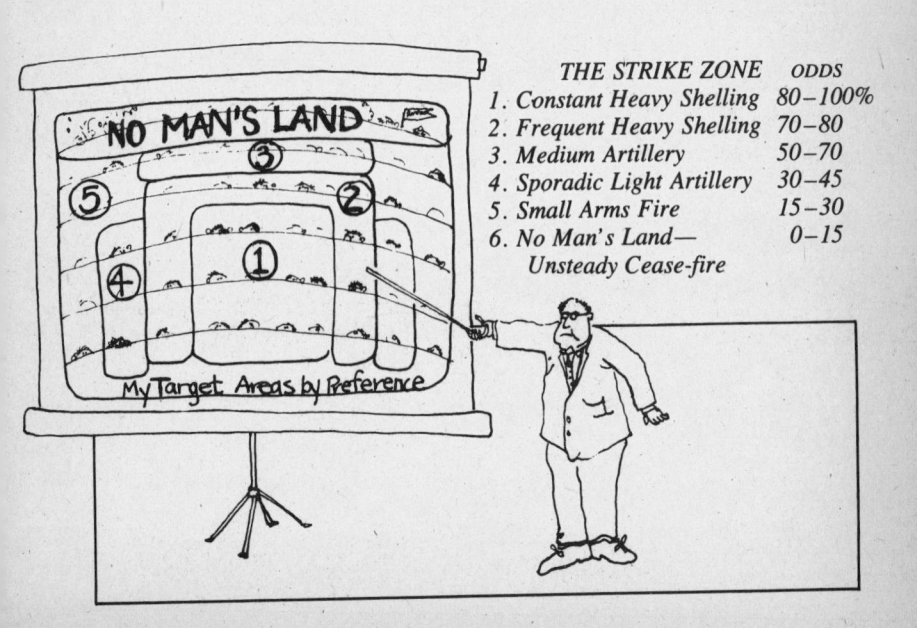

THE STRIKE ZONE	ODDS
1. Constant Heavy Shelling	80–100%
2. Frequent Heavy Shelling	70–80
3. Medium Artillery	50–70
4. Sporadic Light Artillery	30–45
5. Small Arms Fire	15–30
6. No Man's Land— Unsteady Cease-fire	0–15

Such knowledge of shelling patterns makes it quite simple to decide where to dig your foxhole; simply assess how much enemy fire you can withstand and still survive.

Constant Heavy Shelling

To sit in this sector, you must be ready to take the heat. You must

1. be completely prepared to brief up to six cases at a time. Every day.
2. have a 100% attendance record, and never be late.
3. have no study aids in class.
4. not only stay awake, but serve as the requisite eager face the prof is searching for whenever he looks up to establish "eye contact" with the class.
5. be prepared for the prof's sexual advances if you are cute and of the opposite sex (or the sex the prof likes).
6. be aware that you are going to be a likely target for Asshole Bingo competition.
7. be ready to take over whenever any other student runs into difficulty.
8. be ready to run up to the prof after class to make some obsequious and self-serving remark.

Frequent Heavy Shelling

This is still a dangerous area, and can actually be the heaviest hit, because frequently the podium obscures the front rows and the third row is actually closest to eye level. So all of the caveats of the former sector apply, although there are some advantages to sitting here. You're

1. not as likely to be called to pick up the slack for somebody who has gotten bogged down in his briefs.
2. not quite as obligated to run down and pant in front of the prof after class.

Medium Artillery

The students in this area, as the prof knows, are likely to be well prepared, but they don't feel the need to be right up front hanging on every word. And they are far enough back to be distracted by the Back-of-the-Bus Gang, and to get away with using canned (or a friend's) briefs every now and then, so they are not a sure bet. In this sector

1. you are close enough to participate, but far enough away to avoid being tyrannized.
2. you will be constantly entertained by the Back-of-the-Bus Gang, who will try to get you to join in the football pool, or job you in as the studio audience in their college bowl series. If you *really* want to hear the prof, sit up closer; in this row, you must be good-humored with the balcony squad. You're on their turf, after all.

Sporadic Light Artillery

This sector would otherwise be the free-fire zone, because you are up so close. But you are out of the prof's direct line of vision, tucked away on either side, and you will benefit from this peripheral seating. As they say, "Out of sight, out of mind."

1. In this area you are subject to stringent restrictions when it comes to canned briefs and un-

disguised snoozing, since you would be in full view should the prof happen to turn his head and address you directly.
2. But he rarely will do so. Thus, this location offers the benefits of proximity to the prof without the liability of a high profile.

Sporadic Small-Arms Fire
These sectors are far enough back or far enough to either side to make them relatively safe from a prof's roving eye. You are far from the madding crowd. You can drift, use study aids (front rows should exercise caution about this), and enjoy what is as close to peace of mind as one can come in a law school class. Liabilities and other features:
1. You really can't hear the prof too well, so your attention is bound to wander if you don't really concentrate.
2. If you are in the back rows, you will be close to the worst offenders of the Back-of-the-Bus Gang and will probably end up betting on horses with them instead of taking notes on the lectures.

No-Man's-Land: Unsteady Cease-Fire with Occasional Highly Accurate Mortar Attacks
Don't ask us why, but the back-row "balcony section" seems to be the bane of law school profs everywhere. It seems to attract the McMurphy's, Machine Gun Marys, Dr. Gonzos, and James Deans of every class. It is, in short, the lair of the dreaded Back-of-the-Bus Gang.

THE BACK-OF-THE-BUS GANG
Fully prepared, Back-of-the-Bus Gang members impatiently wait for class to begin.

What is it that lures the Wild Bunch to this distant and elevated plateau? Is it that they enjoy the fact that because of the angle, the prof can't see their beers? Or do they appreciate being able to concentrate on handicapping the various races and sports events they are betting on without being disturbed?

Until recently, their motivation remained elusive, because scouts sent up there to report never returned. But through diligence and deception we have finally obtained the analysis of a noted anthropologist who infiltrated their ranks disguised as a potted palm.

☐ THE BACK-OF-THE-BUS GANG: A View from the Rear

Contrary to professors' inferences, the members of the Back-of-the-Bus Gang do not choose their balcony section out of fear of having to speak out in class. Far from it. They are usually some of the brightest kids in the class, and when their turns come up, will show off their legal acumen with aplomb. It is just they prefer being the *bête noirs* in a flock of human sheep.

Secure in the knowledge that classroom performance has no effect on grades (in law school, your final exam *is* your grade—forget about those *Paper Chase* reruns), members of the BB Gang see no reason to engage in the Socratic song-and-dance. In fact, they are amazed to see that the other students do so in deadly earnest, as this eventually creates an aura of terrifying importance around a ritual the gang sees as silly at best and humiliating at worst.

In protest, they eventually become a pain in the posterior to the prof, as their obvious disdain for the Socratic method and generally insubordinate techniques (designed to evade questions) inevitably turn the whole process into a gag fest.

The professor will react much the way one would expect. Initially, he will attempt to embarrass these hooligans into submission. These attempts are doomed to failure because they will cheerfully admit they're not prepared, and will instead use the opportunity to fire off a few witty rejoinders. After this initial assault, the prof will generally avoid calling on the gang, as he tends to lose yardage each time he makes a foray up there. He will, however, learn their individual names and make "discipline calls" on the offending members whenever the gang has become too boisterous.

Despite their apparent absorption in self-amusement, the merry pranksters in the back of the bus are not without a sense of obligation to the professor and class. They *do* feel obligated: primarily to entertain everybody within earshot as much as possible through remarks, impromptu skits, College Bowl series, and generally indefensible behavior, but also

☐ to pass on hot tips from their more extensive experience in sports handicapping.

☐ to stall the professor for the last

seven minutes of class whenever it is clear that the Prof wants to cover another case (and the rest of the class doesn't).
- [ ] to pass around pornographic briefs and caricatures of the prof.
- [ ] to ease the tension in the room by loudly opening their beer pop-tops at the proper dramatic moments.
- [ ] to come up with increasingly clever ways to deflect the prof's questions while setting up somebody else for the fall.
- [ ] to engage the prof in verbal volleyball, luring him into trading witticisms, then destroying him with a terrific quips, thus Groucho Marxing his authority; and to contribute in numerous creative ways to the festive classroom atmosphere that makes a professor wonder why he ever took up teaching, and makes the students wonder why they ever took up law.

Conscientious gang members study advance sheet reports of recent developments in criminal law.

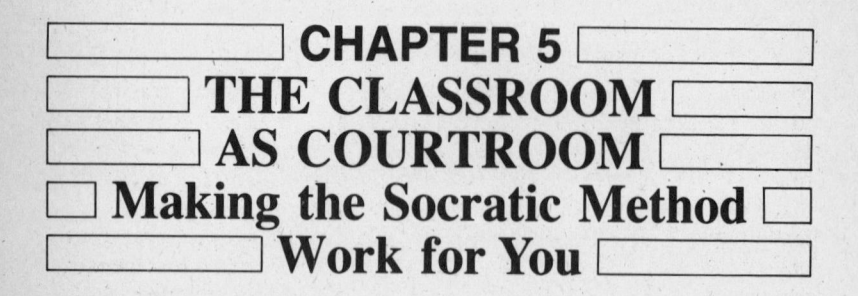

CHAPTER 5
THE CLASSROOM AS COURTROOM
Making the Socratic Method Work for You

You've studied all night. Your sleep was fitful, tormented. And now, as if by some internal perversity, your mind has jumbled all of those lucid cases into a chaotic mass. You can't even recall the question posed a moment ago. The blurry image of your professor sways in front of you, grinning in sadistic anticipation. Your palms are sweating. You tremble imperceptibly, fighting the urge to lose your breakfast. It is deadly silent all around you. You struggle to find your voice, to focus your attention. Your brain races, searching for something—anything—coherent to say. You pray for more time, just a few more minutes—but this is it.

It's time to get out of bed. Otherwise, you're going to be late for your 9:00 a.m. class.

Nonstudents can't possibly understand why the prospect of going to class fills the legal neophyte with the same sense of enthusiasm and anticipation as that of a six-year-old who has been strapped to the dentist's chair. Words like "unpleasant" and "ghastly" can't convey the full ethos of the experience. Because, in a real sense, the classroom you are about to enter is a courtroom, and you are the defendant. And there is a hanging judge and a surly jury waiting to feed you to the lions.

☐ THE CASEBOOK METHOD

Despite criticism, controversy, and, in one documented case, threatened extermination of a poodle, the casebook method has remained the accepted mode of teaching at all major law schools. Why the casebook method? This question was most recently posed to the dean of Harvard Law School, whose answer succinctly summed up the various conflicting rationales: "Because we say so."

Here we discuss how you can emerge unscathed (with just a clawmark here or there) from this classroom - as - Coliseum - as - kangaroo-court and still have time to work on mixing metaphors as badly as we do in this paragraph. First, a little background.

☐ THE SOCRATIC METHOD: A Sordid Overview

Modern civilization owes so much to ancient Greece. The list is endless—Homer, Plato, feta cheese, olives—but the most important gift that the Greeks gave law school professors was a system of philosophical inquiry that would enable them to get straight to the point of a problem without, as Wittgenstein put it, "a lot of fooling around."

When presented with this elegant, lucid system, law school professors everywhere breathed a simultaneous sigh of admiration for its originator, and then unanimously rejected the whole system (which was based entirely on logic) in favor of the Socratic method (which was based entirely on Abbott & Costello).

History

The Socratic method originated in 431 A.D.* on a balmy night in Athens, as Socrates and his pupils sat out in the Plaka passing around a cheap bottle of retsina. Trikinosis (not one of Socrates' brightest pupils) leaned forward, looked into his master's eyes, and earnestly asked, "Socrates, you have taught us that 'Freedom without a hearing is not freedom,' which makes sense, but I must ask, 'What is freedom?'"

*The author is too lazy to look up this date, so it may very well be off by several hundred years.

Then he leaned back in his chair, smiling smugly, before letting out a belch that knocked two disciples flat on their backs.

Socrates was caught completely off guard, as he believed Trikinosis was going to ask him for some change to get another souvlaki. In the past, Trikinosis' questions had all revolved around who was going to pick up the check, or at most, where to get a Mod haircut.

Hence, the master was taken aback. He searched his memory. True, last night he had proclaimed, "Friedman without herring is not Friedman," but he doubted that Trikinosis had heard it, as the latter had already skipped out on the check. No, Triki was trying to be Mr. Smarty Pants, no doubt about it.

So putting on his most thoughtful face, Socrates paused dramatically, then said, "Trikinosis, let me answer it this way. What do *you* think freedom is?" Now *Trikinosis* was suddenly on the spot. Everybody turned toward him expectantly—even the waiters stopped talking and leaned over to hear. Trikinosis, faced with all of this sudden attention, did what any student would do when his most profound and unsolvable question is taken by the professor and thrown back in his face—he turned completely red, gagged, and excused himself to go to the bathroom. And to this day, the Socratic method has remained unchanged. (And so has Friedman, if you want to know the truth).

Modern Use: The Professor's Tool

The Socratic method (S/M) has

emerged as the single most popular teaching tool among law school professors. For a teacher skilled in the art of S/M there are many advantages. Most important, it enables the professor to exercise discipline in class; through skillful use of the wide variety of available S/M devices, a prof can keep students in a submissive role, thereby retaining his or her dominant position.

As any professor will tell you, the S/M ordeal eventually leads to a common bondage between the students. This bondage is critical, because, although the students have implicitly consented to submit to S/M in advance, some may try to defect when the going gets rough. Common bondage and discipline ties them to other students and restrains them from escaping before the S/M session is over.

S/M: The Ultimate Weapon

The thrill of domination is not the only benefit that S/M affords a professor. There is also the luxurious feeling of security that comes from possessing a system that enables him to rule without resorting to intelligent thought—much like President Reagan's 3×5 cue cards. Once a prof has mastered S/M, he can teach any law school subject. He does not have to know *anything* about the case, or about the subject, for that matter. In fact, he doesn't even have to know what city he's in.

Through S/M, a prof can come into class with his brain a complete *tabula rasa* and find out everything

*GEAT MOMENTS IN LEGAL HISTORY
Socrates invents the Socratic Method and beats the check— all in the same meal.*

he needs to know from the students while ostensibly "teaching" them.

In one case, an NYU Law School professor went on a transcontinental bender, woke up in a Civil Procedure class at Stanford, and successfully interrogated, bullied, and S/Med his students into teaching themselves three cases.

At *no* point did the professor offer *any* information. He simply "asked questions," and "demanded detailed explanations." If a student did this, he would be considered a moron. But this particular prof immediately got a reputation as a "demanding perfectionist" and was given instant tenure, which he turned down because he was already working full-time in the garment district.

This is why law school profs can switch subjects, "teaching" each with equal facility. Because once you have mastered S/M, any factual knowledge you have becomes irrelevant. In fact, purists maintain that knowledge cramps their interrogating style. Hence the professorial adage "A little learning is a dangerous thing."

Of course, this rhetorical gravy train relies heavily on the preparedness of the students. What happens if the students aren't prepared? What happens when the professor calls on one, two, three students consecutively, and each of them passes? What if he calls for volunteers and no one volunteers? What does he do then?

Right. He walks out.

He snorts contemptuously, gives the class a withering look of scorn, then dramatically exits, throwing some remark over his shoulder like "Come back when you want to learn law. I'm not going to waste my time."

It really is a beautiful racket. And foolproof, too.

Beats working!

☐ ESCAPING FROM S/M: How to Pass with Class

Admittedly, with all of this armor, our modern-day professional Goliath looks hard to beat. But a closer look reveals several chinks in the breastplate, a few thinly disguised openings, and at least three Achilles heels (which in itself is kind of remarkable). The professor's first weakness is created by the very same obsequious behavior he has worked so hard to inculcate in his students. Because the class laughs uproariously at his most feeble attempts at humor, he fancies himself something of a wag. This makes him vulnerable, as he can be lured into repartee by a quick-witted escape artist. In the ensuing "Battle of Bon Mots" the student will usually escape, because once the prof takes off his legal armor and tries to match epées, he is invariably outclassed. And if he loses the war of wits, he can't then try to recapture the offender and reexert his S/M authority by saying, "Enough kidding. Now about this case..." because it will be seen as sour grapes.

Your repartee does not even have to be brilliant (although, of course, it would be preferable if it were). Your classmates are nervous enough to laugh at anything, and are probably inured to the professor's mediocre humor by the second day, so you don't have to be Noel Coward to pull off an escape. Also, each of your fellow students has been on the firing-line at one time or other, so they sympathize with your attempts to hit the "eject" button.

It is a documented fact that all of your peers appreciate a creative escape act if it is done with finesse; they admire the recklessness and daring, and will immortalize the successful escapee in subsequent song, story, and, most important, gossip.

"I PASS" AS A CONCEPT

Nonlawyers confuse passing *in* class with passing *the* class. It would be terrific if this were true; a student could then guarantee his graduation simply by saying "I pass" whenever asked a question. Unfortunately, passing *in* class and passing *the* class seem to be mutually exclusive in law school: The more a student says "I pass," the more the professor wants to flunk him.

In our opinion, professors are justified in their wish to torpedo any student who says "I pass" in class. It shows that the student (1) is too cowardly to try to wing it, and (2) lacks sufficient creativity to come up with a debonair response which would provide the necessary levity to the encounter, enabling the prof to come out smelling like a rose.

When you think about it, this is one of the few moments in class which does provide a chance for hilarity. And contrary to what you may think, a prof does not wish to have his class branded as dull (*hard*, yes, but not dull). So don't disappoint him. You'll find that he will reward you by calling on you only infrequently, when the crowd needs perking up.

Here are some traditional favorite ways to "pass with class":

1. "I'd like to demurrer on account of the facts I have on this case do not constitute a cause of Brief." (Try to do this with a Damon Runyon accent - they love it!)
2. "I'm afraid I will have to take the fifth on that, because if I open my mouth it will incriminate me."
3. "Having thoroughly examined all the facts in this case, I have

reached a conclusion. I'm punting."
4. "Beam me up, Scotty!"
5. "Warp 9, Sulu!"
6. "I ought to preface my analysis of this case by saying that I have not read any of the facts. However, it's clear that—" (At this point you will be cut off by the prof.)
7. "So sorry, *no hablo inglés, señor.*"
8. "Gee, I'd love to cover that case, but Mr. Russo here [or whoever is sitting next to you] worked so hard preparing it last night that I feel kind of obligated to let him take it. All yours, Jimmy!" (*See also* "The lateral.")
9. "Listen. Ordinarily I'd grab this opportunity. But I'm so upset over our foreign policy at the moment that I can't even think straight."

VARIATIONS ON A THEME: Passing With Class, Part II

The Screen
Take some aspect of the case and go immediately into some off-the-wall personal story which will amuse the class, embarrass the prof, and convince everybody you're crazy.

Example: "I couldn't help noticing that this case is *Hilton Hotels* vs. *Somebody or other*, and I've got to tell you, I spent a couple of weeks at the Grand Hawaiian in Honolulu and you know what? It's overrated. I mean, sure the Tiki Room is nice with the fake lava waterfall and those inflated puffer fish, but I can't believe the pu-pu platter costs $12.95 and you only get one egg roll and some gross shrimp and this poi stuff, which is like library paste, but anyway, there was this Huki Lau band with *real ukeleles...*"

The Bomb ("Policy" argument)
If you have a vague idea about the facts of the case, try to immediately elevate it to the metaphysical. Then you can comfortably argue cosmic generalities until the prof tears himself away (unless you're attending Yale, in which case you are engaging in the normal approach to a case and should not rely on this technique if you want to bail out).

Example: "This is a divorce action. You know, it's alarming how many people get divorced these days. Over 50%. One can only wonder whether easy access to divorce courts is actually causing this. I mean, obviously the people are unhappy, but maybe if they knew that there was no easy way out they would try to make it work. It's like the statute of frauds; if we got rid of that, then oral contracts would be given more credibility and honor would replace voluminous merger clauses and signatures. What do you think?"

The Reverse
So you haven't read this case. But you just heard the last one. You may have even taken notes (in short, you are prepared for the previous case). So discuss it. Pick some point from the previous case and hammer it to death. "Before we get into this case, I'd like to go back to something that was bothering me about the one we just finished...."

The Mini-screen

"I had a product under warranty just like the plantiff in the facts of the last case. It was a blender and it had a limited warranty, and it didn't last for two months. Of course, I used it to mix some incredible iced drinks; the ice cubes may have done it—piña coladas, mai tais, golden Cadillacs—do you know what goes into a golden Cadillac? It's really quite good. The key is you take creme de cocão..."

The Lateral

This is actually a form of punting. You start off confidently with a small speech, and then, without warning, pass the whole mess to the student to your left or right. You're guaranteed a big laugh and you're off the hook, but your seatmate will spend the rest of the year trying to assassinate you, so you should evaluate the pros and cons before proceding with this one.

In one cute variation, the lateral is made to any student who had his hand up for the previous case. (This crossover technique can augment your Asshole Bingo score—you frame the "asshole" highest on your bingo card. If the prof bites, the asshole will have to answer at least six questions, thus filling out your card. (*See* "Asshole Bingo—A Law School Tradition" in the next chapter.)

Example: "Why yes. I'd be glad to discuss this case. But before I begin, I should point out that my co-counsel Mr. Egan was up all night preparing this case, and has done such a wonderful job that I really must defer. Take it away, Bobby!"

The Four-eyed Monster

This is a multipurpose strategy, and combines easily, in part or completely, with all other techniques we've discussed.

1. **Civil pro:** "When the defendant wants to contest subject matter jurisdiction, does he bear the burden of guessing whether the court will hold that he has submitted to in personam jurisdiction by doing so?" (This issue has yet to be resolved in any jurisdiction, so it can always be tagged on when you want to camouflage your pass.)

2. **Outrage:** "Do you mean to tell me that it is okay to take somebody's *blood* for evidence? And that doesn't shock the conscience of the court? My God, what does it *take*?" (Most professors would rather not deal with someone who is obviously too emotional to hold a rational discussion.)

3. **Confidential:** "Just between us, don't you think that the court was looking for any way to find for the defendant? Their reasoning is a little strained, wouldn't you agree? I mean, I sympathize with the defendant, too, but do you really think the facts merit the kind of ruling that the court came up with?"

Stalling for Time

This technique is effective only when there are five minutes or less left of class time. Stalling for time is the equivalent of waiting for the clock to run out. You give the prof every indication that you have no intention of answering him. He will attempt to wring it out of you (if he is in a good mood), but will eventually lose interest and leave you alone, by which time class will be over and you will be free to leave.

PROF: Could you please give the class the facts on this case?
STUD: Sure. Which case are we talking about?
PROF: The one directly following the case we just discussed.
STUD: Oh, you mean *Hanson* v. *Denckla*?
PROF: Yes. That is the case we just discussed.
STUD: You know, I'm still bothered by something in that last—
PROF: You can ask me after class. I'm interested in this case.
STUD: Oh, me too. It's a very interesting case.
PROF: Right. So why don't you tell the class a little about it?
STUD: Sure. What would they like to know about it?
PROF: Well, counselor, why don't we start with the facts, hmm?
STUD: Certainly. By "facts" you don't mean all of the facts, right? Just the relevant ones.
PROF: You are a genius.
STUD: Thank you.

PROF: So I take it that you are entirely unprepared for this case?
STUD: It depends—what do you mean by entirely unprepared?
PROF: You have not prepared a brief.
STUD: Well, not in the formal sense.
PROF: You don't have a clue about this case.
STUD: Well, that's easy for *you* to say. You wrote the casebook.
PROF: Why do you bother coming to class?
STUD: Beats working.
PROF: Here is a dime. Please call your mother and tell her—
STUD: Um, listen, my mom lives in California. I'm going to need more change. Anybody have $2.35 in change? Wait—I found some more quarters. Anybody have $1.25?

By now the bell should have rung. If not, class is shot anyway, so you're safe.

Razzle-Dazzle

When you have the luxury of being truly prepared, why plunge in earnestly like everyone else? Have a little fun first. Fake a punt, and then when the prof begins to abuse you, surprise him with a comprehensive brief. The prof will either be pleasantly surprised that you're prepared, or incensed that you wasted his time. Either way, you will have won that particular Socratic skirmish—and each win counts in this game.

CHAPTER 6
DIVERTISSEMENTS
Games to Keep You Awake In Class

The law school classroom, after years of evolution, has become a perfect educational environment. The gracefully curved amphitheater, the mellifluous drone of your professor berating hapless students, the cozy ambiance of central heating, the soft, fluorescent lighting designed to reduce glare—all these factors combine to create an ideal setting—for a nice, long nap.

However, because professors inevitably take light snoring as a personal affront, and because of the disorientation one feels when one goes to sleep in Civil Procedure and wakes up in Law of the Sea two days later, we are providing a list of amusing and instructive games that can be played (indeed, can *only* be played) in class, to keep the sandman from your door. They are gleaned from a small, leather-bound volume recently unearthed at Cornell Law School, which contained a list of the favorite divertissements enjoyed by that school's most famous Back-of-the-Bus gang (1924).

Before we delve into Funland, however, let us examine the underlying Weltschmerz that creates the requisite atmosphere of tension so necessary to high-level competitions.

Playing Catch-Up
The most fundamentally distressing realization that is forced upon a first-year fledgling usually occurs within the first three weeks of school (normally just following the discovery that his roommate is opposed to any form of personal hygiene for religious reasons). After attempting to stay abreast of every class, assiduously briefing, studying, and taking notes for about two weeks, he comes to the horrifying recognition that he is falling behind—despite his 20-hour-a-day schedule, despite working weekends, despite his liberal use of amphetamines and willingness to allow his body to become wracked with vitamin-D-deficiency diseases from lack of sunshine. He is falling *behind*!

After the waves of inevitable blind panic and existential nausea inspired by this epiphany subside, our student can now analyze the Handwriting on the Wall with as much cold, reasonable detachment as can be mustered by someone in an advanced state of shock—and this is what he sees:

"You can be prepared for *some* of your classes *all* of the time; you can be prepared for *all* of your classes *some* of the time; but you can't be prepared for *all* of your classes *all* of the time."

Once he can objectively assess this truism, the student suddenly perceives a vast panoply of options opening in front of him. First, of course, there is suicide. But that's tacky, and besides, it's a felony, and you can't be admitted to the bar with a felony on your record. So that's out.

Then it hits him. Countless morons have made it through law school before him, and they could not possibly have been doing more work, so they must have been—taking *chances*!

They were playing the odds, preparing full, formal briefs in classes where they *knew* they would be called on, but forgoing heavy briefing in classes where they felt safe to just show up ready to take notes.

Our student is right, of course. For generations, law students have relied on the "stride, glide, and let it slide" technique, leapfrogging classes (you are *never* equally prepared and confident in *all* of your classes at the *same* time) until finals, when they attempt to bring all their courses in, nose-to-nose, at the wire.

Since each and every student is engaged in this deft juggling act, a collective paranoia is created, centered around the likelihood of being subjected to "The Call of the Wild" in any given class.

10 Little Indians: Who's Next

Because the dubious honor of being selected for the S/M ordeal is such a harrowing experience, students rightly spend most of their study time trying to figure out who will be chosen as the professor's next victims. Strategists attempt to pattern each prof's Standard Operating Procedure, with the aim of predicting where, when, and how often the prof will strike, and how long he will generally sustain an attack.

For this reason, good handicappers are in great demand, because they are worth their weight in peace of mind. And, of course, they are *invaluable* in Asshole Bingo competition.

☐ ASSHOLE BINGO

No one is sure just where this popular game originated, but it is a huge favorite at law schools across the country, largely due to the vast supply of qualified participants. Asshole Bingo combines bingo skills, handicapping abilities, and character assassination in an intellectually challenging, emotionally satisfying board game that can be played simultaneously by up to 30 players.

EQUIPMENT

1. **Card.** Each player must have an Asshole Bingo Card in order to

play. The Asshole Bingo Card can be purchased at fine stores everywhere, but serious players make their own. The board consists of 16 squares. Two of the squares are already-filled-in "free" squares. Their locations change with each game.* They are *never* in the same row.

2. Assholes. Before commencing the game, each player must select four of his fellow students and list them on his card. They will be called—for lack of a more accurate word—"Assholes."

*The Official Asshole Bingo Card comes with the free squares already marked out. In informal Asshole Bingo, each player marks out two before the game begins.

Fig. 1

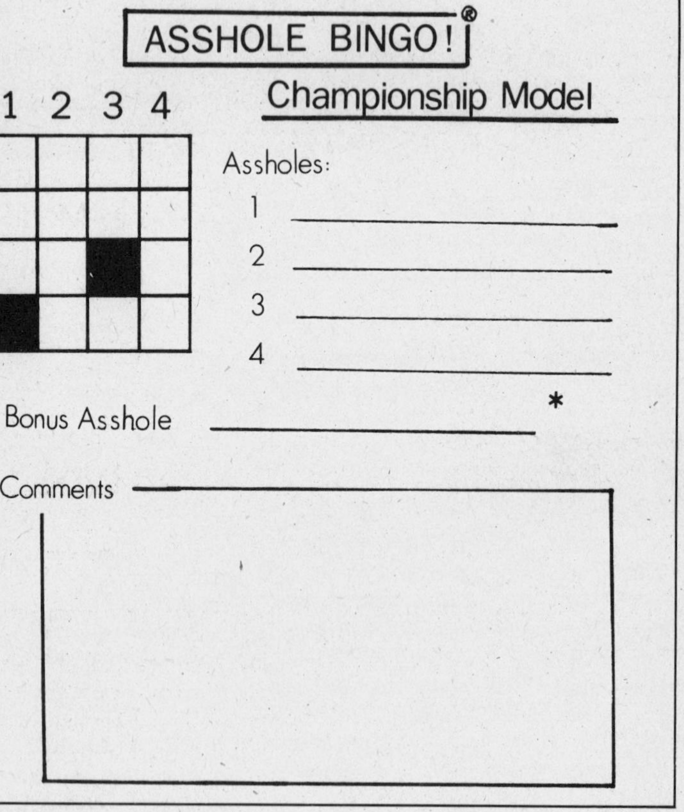

ASSHOLE BINGO!®
Championship Model

Assholes:
1 _____
2 _____
3 _____
4 _____

Bonus Asshole _____ *

Comments

HOW TO SELECT ASSHOLES FOR THE DAY

Here is where the handicapping comes in. Each Asshole is chosen based on the likelihood that he will speak out in class, either because he volunteered by raising his hand or because he was called on by the professor to cover a case. List the Assholes from "most likely to speak out several times" to "next most likely," etc. A player may not select himself.

HOW TO PLAY

1. After selecting and prioritizing Assholes, fill in the 14 open squares with their names.

   List the main Asshole 5 times,
   the next Asshole 4 times,
   the next Asshole 3 times,
   and the last Asshole 2 times.

You should have one alternate Asshole listed on your card who is, in essence, a "wild card" and can be inserted anywhere when he speaks out. (See Fig. 2.) This "Bonus Asshole" can wrest victory from the jaws of defeat by filling in a critical blank.

Note: Free squares cannot be adjoining. No more than two identical initials (i.e. same Asshole) may be placed in the same row.

2. Each time one of the four Assholes speaks up in class, blacken one of the squares containing his initial (Fig. 3). (*Note: Passes*

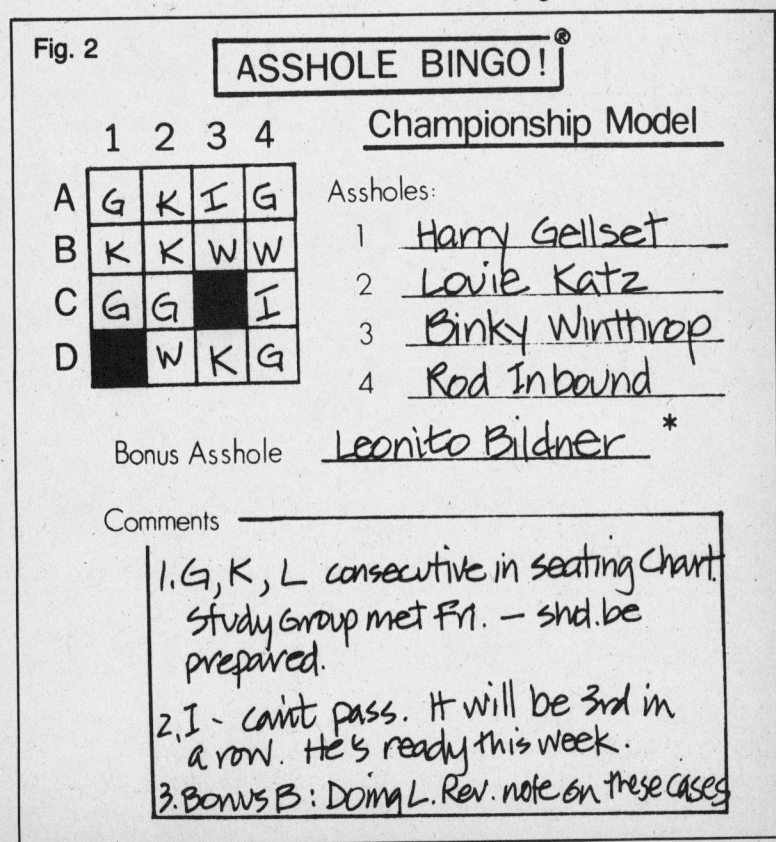

Fig. 2

ASSHOLE BINGO!®

Championship Model

	1	2	3	4
A	G	K	I	G
B	K	K	W	W
C	G	G	■	I
D	■	W	K	G

Assholes:
1. Harry Gellset
2. Louie Katz
3. Binky Winthrop
4. Rod Inbound

Bonus Asshole Leonito Bildner *

Comments

1. G, K, L consecutive in seating chart. Study Group met Fri. — shd. be prepared.
2. I — can't pass. It will be 3rd in a row. He's ready this week.
3. Bonus B: Doing L. Rev. note on these cases

don't count, but *attempted* answers do, even if the answer is wrong.)

Example: Gellset is asked to brief the case. He *passes*! No mark.

Prof asks for volunteers. Katz volunteers, reads brief. Blacken in one K.

Prof asks quick question of Binky Winthrop, who was napping. She answers. Another question, another answer. Blacken in two Ws.

3. When you have achieved a filled-in straight line (either horizontal, vertical, or diagonal), immediately call "BINGO!" in a clear, resonant voice. (See Fig. 4.)

Binky stalls, prof turns the question back to Louie to resume discussion. Louie answers! BINGO!

This will cause immediate pandemonium in class, because everybody knows what game you are playing. It will also humiliate the unfortunate Asshole, because even the professor is aware of this classic game. There is nowhere to run, nowhere to hide.

4. Unlike regular Bingo, this game continues until there is a first-, second-, and third-place winner (sometimes the same competitor makes a clean sweep!), or until the professor threatens to have all of the competitors arrested.

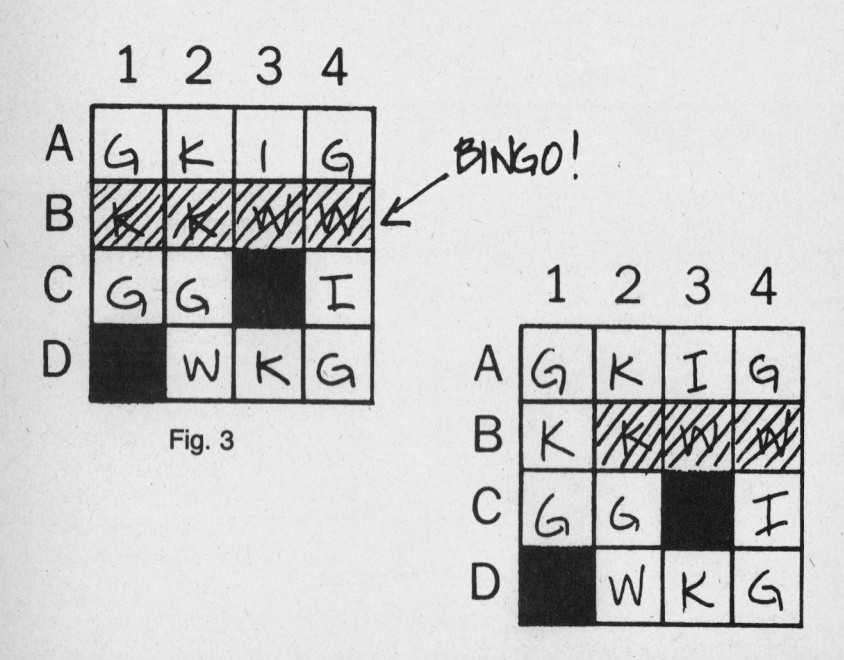

Fig. 3

Fig. 4

DIVERTISSEMENTS ☐ 51

GREAT MOMENTS IN ASSHOLE BINGO HISTORY
An elated Robin displays her winning Bingo combinaton as admirers look on. The winning square was scored when Asshole Rodney Skikos volunteered for the second time. Ann, who was expecting Rod to pass, cannot hide her disappointment.

☐ COLLEGE BOWL

Like its TV counterpart, this game is a great crowd-pleaser, rewarding quick wits and quick hands. The only difference between law school College Bowl and TV College Bowl is that in law school College Bowl

1. the questions are supplied by the professor, *not* the moderator, and are all based on law, and
2. the professor has no idea whatsoever that the game is being played (this ensures his lack of bias).

Players
There is one moderator, and up to eight players. To guarantee unhampered play, it is important that all players be situated far enough back in the room to allow the moderator to talk loudly to the studio audience, without the professor hearing. Thus, most College Bowl games are played by—you guessed it—the Back-of-the-Bus Gang.

Equipment
As this game features individual rather than team competition, each player should have his or her own "College Bowl" placard with name and college boldly inscribed thereon. In addition, each player should have a small hotel bell-captain's bell to ring at the moment he anticipates the answer to the professor's question.

52 □ ONE-L: THE RITES (AND WRONGS) OF PASSAGE

In some jurisdictions, bells are not used because they are too loud (remember, you don't want to disturb the prof) and small "flatulence bags" are substituted. The moderator should have an old 1950s news microphone.

Playing the Game
As the professor "discusses" a case by posing question after question, the moderator (who should be a College Bowl veteran) simultaneously narrates the game, identifies upcoming questions, and assigns point values.

PROF: So the defendant, who is a resident of Nebraska, is...
MODERATOR: (Folks, Harvard blew that last question, but it looks
PROF: ...being sued by a New York plaintiff in a New...
MODERATOR: like he'll have a chance to bounce back because
PROF: ...York court. The accident occurred in New...
MODERATOR: we have a conflicts question coming up, worth 15 points.)
PROF: ...Jersey. In what court can the plaintiff properly...

COLLEGE BOWL WITH THE BACK-OF-THE-BUS GANG
Faced with an Interpleader question, which the moderator had designated as a 15-pointer, enthusiastic College Bowl competitors vie discreetly for the Professor's attention.

MODERATOR: (For 15 points!)
PROF: ... bring suit?

At this point, the action is much like TV's College Bowl. The competitors slam their hands down on their respective bells or buzzers and wave their hands eagerly. But the difference here is that the *professor*, not the moderator, picks the lucky contestant. If the contestant answers the question correctly, he is usually given follow-up questions by the prof until he makes a mistake.

At this point, the moderator sounds a buzzer and offers the question to the other contestants who are raising their hands. Again, the professor picks the follow-up competitor!

PROF: Yes, Mr. Weidemann?
MODERATOR: (Harvard gets the nod for the 15-pointer.)
HARVARD: Because the defendant is being the most inconvenienced, he is the party who should be able to dictate the forum.
PROF: That is the stupidest thing I've ever heard. Can...
MODERATOR: (Ding! Minus 15 for Harvard. Can you
PROF: ... anyone here help Mr. Weidemann out? Mr. Brilltex?
MODERATOR: take it, Cornell?)
CORNELL: As the court noted, the plaintiff chooses the forum in this case.
PROF: Correct. And could he have brought it in Nebraska?
MODERATOR: (15 points for Cornell, and a 5-point bonus question!)
CORNELL (ASIDE): Would you shut the hell up, Coochie? I'm trying to concentrate, for Chrissake!

MODERATOR: (Cornell is rattled, folks—looks like he'll punt this one.)
PROF: I beg your pardon Mr. Brilltex?

As indicated College Bowl can be properly played only in classes where the moderator can carry on outside of the professor's earshot. Under the ideal circumstances, moderator adjusts his volume so that he can be heard by everyone except the front two rows (and, obviously, the professor). This enables him to narrate the College Bowl simultaneously as the prof speaks. It also enables him to heckle the competitors while they are drawing fire from the professor, providing the requisite tension for good College Bowl competition.

To avoid favoritism, the professor should never know when College Bowl is in session. (Although the name tags and bell-captain buzzers will raise his suspicions that something is afoot—to say nothing of the sudden burst of enthusiastic handraising from the back of the class.) If it is clear that he suspects something (i.e., if he says, "You punks think you're pretty cute back there, don't you?") then switch promptly to the more discreet entertainment offered by Asshole Bingo.

☐ **FOOTBALL POOL**

This is a regular football pool, with a list of the week's competing teams together with their point spreads. Competitors receive the list through locker mail, delivered by the local first-year student/bookie (usually a New Yorker). To play, you simply choose your teams, then submit your sheet (with the dollar entrance fee) to the bookie before the deadline. For maximum enjoyment this game should be played during Property class early in the week. Since you have the sports section of the paper with all of the official point spreads and can confer with fellow competitors while the information is fresh, the overall quality of betting is enhanced. And, needless to say, so is Property class.

☐ BEAT THE CLOCK

This is a challenging game pitting the wits of the student against those of the professor. It is played whenever discussion of a case ends with five minutes of class (or less) left on the clock. In the slight pause following the discussion of the last case, just before the professor launches into a new one, the competitor raises his hand. (Note: This act of volunteering distinguishes "Beat the Clock" from "Stalling for Time". In the latter, you have already been called on—it is a defensive maneuver, whereas "Beat the Clock" is, by any definition, offensive.)

The competitor will, through seemingly earnest queries, attempt to stall the prof until time runs out and class must be dismissed. This is an exciting game that can be played by individual competitors or teams.

Some terrific one-on-one competition occurs later in the season when the professors take on students who they know from past experience are expert stallers. Some professors deliberately end discussions of cases with seven minutes to go, just to tempt the Beat the Clock gang out into the open. The ensuing parry and thrust is nothing short of inspiring.

☐ BOGUS BRIEFS:
The Glickfeld Reporter

Churned out by the frustrated creative writers of the class, the *Glickfeld Reporter*, named for the master of bogus brief-writing (U. of Chicago Law, '37), consists of an ever-expanding series of briefs covering very important fictitious cases, including *Shirley Spano v. Two Medium-Sized Aloha Party Shirts*, *Ray-Ban v. Ban-Lon v. Won Ton Ton*, and others. For your reading pleasure, we have obtained some recent *Glickfeld Reporter* advance sheets, containing a Second Circuit case (Columbia Law School), wherein the court dealt emphatically with, among other issues, the constitutionality of Howard Cosell.

SPANO V. TWO MEDIUM-SIZED ALOHA PARTY SHIRTS
Facts
Defendant was a 32-year-old kindergarten teacher. Her hobbies were knitting, cooking, jogging, and running machine guns to Libya.

On the Friday night in question, she heard a knock at the door. When she asked who it was, a voice called out, "9-G? Large gefiltefish, pig's knuckles, and corned beef on rye with extra ketchup, relish, and Worcestershire sauce?" This raised the defendant's suspicions, since she normally ordered the aforementioned sandwich only on bulky rolls. But she opened the door.

She was instantly knocked unconscious by a sudden, loud blast of Mariachi music from a hand-held portable stereo. The police burst in, wearing incredibly loud Hawaiian party shirts and Bermuda shorts. Defendant, terrified that her home was being invaded by fat tourists from Ohio, locked herself in the bathroom and refused to come out until Officer A coaxed her out with an offer of Pralines 'n' Cream ice cream, her favorite. To her chagrin, she discovered that it was, in fact, Butter Brickle. The officers ransacked the house (particularly the refrigerator) looking for evidence, or, failing that, a few cold beers. Their search turned up two six-packs of Mickey Big Mouths, of which two bottles were opened. Officer B told defendant of the penalties for open containers, and over defendant's hysterical protestations, turned on the TV to Monday Night Football.

At the sight of Howard Cosell, defendant screamed and began a lengthy confession, using props and sight gags. Officers A and B told her to "stow it, for Chrissake, until halftime." As a result, defendant was forced to endure almost two quarters of trying dialogue between Howard Cosell and Dandy Don.

During all times in question, the police refused to share the potato chips. They hogged the couch, and refused to pay up, even though the defendant won the football pool. Furthermore, despite repeated requests by defendant, they refused to remove their Hawaiian party shirts. At halftime, after listening to about four minutes of defendant's confession, they decided it was too boring and left without cleaning up.

Issue
Was the police's warrantless search unreasonable?

Holding
Any search in which defendant is subjected to two quarters of Howard Cosell is unreasonable as a matter of law.

Rationale
While exigencies may justify an otherwise unconstitutional search, there are some rights that are so fundamental that if the police violate them, the search becomes unreasonable *per se*, and all evidence seized may not be offered in court, but must be given to Kaufman's Wholesale Carpet Supply to be used verbatim in their advertisements. While the officers' method of gaining entry to defendant's apartment was constitutionally permissible under the "Mariachi Boom Box" exception, once they were inside, they were obligated to recognize that defendant believed that their subsequent

requests of her were made "under color of Law" (in this case, tropical colors not seen since Filmore East stopped producing black-light posters) and thus defendant felt compelled to watch the football game with them, taking the point spread and betting on Dallas even though she was sure the Oakland pass-rush would stop the Cowboys in third-and-long situations. Similarly, she felt that she had no choice in listening to Howard Cosell, even though doing so caused her to break out into a severe rash, which took two weeks to subside. The court held that defendant was thus subjected to Howard against her will—a *per se* constitutional violation.

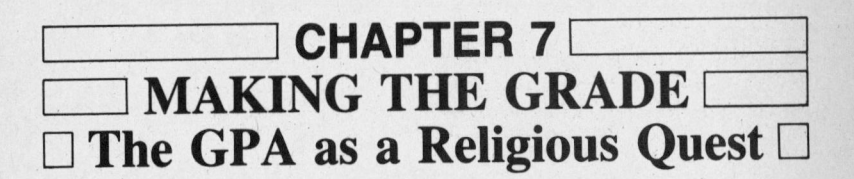

CHAPTER 7
MAKING THE GRADE
The GPA as a Religious Quest

In Molière's day, theater criticism was quick and dirty: If the King applauded at the finale, the play was a success, and the play (and the playwright) would thrive. However, if the King did *not* applaud, that was it—the rest of the crowd could be roaring in a standing ovation and throwing money on the stage, but it didn't matter. The review was in, and it spelled "demise" (in French, of course). Neither the play nor the playwright would ever be heard from again.

Well, mercifully, times have changed for playwrights.* But not for you. If the professor applauds your efforts on your final exam on judgment day, you are speeding on the fast track to Nirvana. If he doesn't, well, we hope you are wearing a seat belt and have a shatterproof windshield. Because just as your GPA and LSAT scores were the only criteria applied by law schools in deciding whether to admit you, your law school GPA (i.e., the grades you achieve on your finals) is the sole criterion applied by law firms in deciding whether to even grant you an interview. This is not to say that if you do well, you will necessarily grab the brass ring and be accepted by the top firm of your choice; it simply means that you have earned a ride on the merry-go-round.

A recent national survey of law firms, conducted by experts in the field, states the case eloquently:

What matters when it comes to granting an interview: GPA, top 10%.

What doesn't matter: anything else.

Conclusion: The secret password entitling a student to a first interview is "top 10% of the class." Some other passwords such as "Gosh, Dad, I'm glad you granted me this interview" and "I should tell you, this gun is loaded" are effective in the right contexts, but there is only one all-purpose ticket to ride: the top 10%. And that means acing

---

*Some off-Broadway producers in New York do not agree with this upbeat assessment. See W. C. Jayroe, "Portrait of the critic as a Fat, Slobbering Tyrant."

all of your exams. Fortunately, this task will be *un morceau de gâteau* if you follow these solid guidelines. They worked for Molière.

This chapter is divided into two sections, "Preparation" and "Taking the exam." Keep in mind that these are very different concepts, much as "preparing to be hit by a truck" and "being hit by a truck" are different concepts.

☐ PRE-LAUNCH PREPARATION

EQUIPMENT
- Outlines
- Study group notes
- Previous year's tests and answers
- Bar review course sample tests and answers
- Mr. Coffee
- Amphetamines, Valium
- Comfortable clothes

PROCEDURE
1. Synthesize the notes you have managed to amass (from friends, your study group, the library trash cans) into something vaguely comprehensible by using commercial outlines
2. Take as many practice tests as you can, using our own patented answer technique (explained below). Learn to underline parties and issues, and to make outlines. This is critical to your success.
3. Don't stay up all night before the exam. If you are up all night in a drugged frenzy and then wander into the exam red-eyed, wearing the same clothes as the night before, it is bound to hurt your chances. Besides, taking an exam in your sweaty tuxedo or fishnets and high heels is uncomfortable and makes your less socially adept peers jealous.

☐ TAKING THE TEST: IRAC AND BEYOND

EQUIPMENT

You have some options here, although some of these items are essential.

Word Processor
The most sensible equipment with which to take a test, obviously, is a word processor with a fully trained legal staff to operate it. But even without the staff, a word processor is a terrific option because you can store an entire casebook, notebook, outline, or what-have-you in its memory bank, and recall it whenever the need arises.

Memory Typewriter
The drawback with a memory typewriter as compared with a word processor is its limited storage capacity. Its advantage is that other student computer "hackers" can't break into your test program and steal the answers.

Electric Typewriter
Make sure it is self-correcting. A prof is duly impressed by a neat, legible exam. Don't worry, he won't read it, he'll just appreciate your gesture and give you an A.

Manual Typewriter
If the electricity goes out, don't

panic—you can either switch to a manual typewriter or plug into the diesel generator you brought.

Diesel Generator
No well-prepared test-taker should be without one. Other students will complain about the noise, but they're just jealous because when the house juice cuts out they're on foot and you're still flying.

Earplugs
These are necessary to screen out unnecessary noise—other typewriters, proctors announcing that time is up, students screaming the Shinto death-cry as they commit ritual harakiri.

360° Mirrors
These can be used both offensively and defensively—to discreetly copy other students' exams and to warn you when a competitive red-hot is about to clip your electric typewriter cord.

Pens
Make sure you take advantage of the 20th century's greatest invention since self-correcting typewriters—erasable pens. They will enable you to change your mind (which you will) in midsentence without having to create a calligraphic dumping site. Remember, teachers are a very aesthetic breed. They don't favor tests that look like Charles Manson's diary.

General rule
Have 10 of everything. If your typewriter screws up or your pen doesn't work, of course any one of your student competitors will cheerfully lend you his typewriter or pen, but just in *case*.

LAW SCHOOL TEST-TAKING TIP #23
Be sure to use your entire body when taking a test—efficient neck-craning can effectively reduce eye-strain

PROCEDURE

For each one-hour question, you should proceed in the following manner.

1. Scan the question fast, *underline* all the parties (especially the ones thrown by Craig Claiborne and Pierre Franey), and get a general feeling about the question, usually vertigo or nausea (30 seconds).
2. Read the question *closely* this time, underlining major issues and listing them on the scrap paper in outline form. Look for any overt references to Ralph Kramden.
3. Outline subissues under major issues. Don't get caught writing a voluminous outline. Nobody sees the outline. And if you don't leave yourself plenty of time—well, you would be amazed by how pathetically brief your test answer looks even if you start writing right away (the James Joyce/Three Stooges technique). If you only turn out a total of two flawless pages (the Ezra Pound minimalist technique), your prof will thank you for sparing him the verbiage, and then flunk you.
4. Start writing with an all-purpose, neutral, canned opening that you have prepared in advance (i.e., for a discussion on Evidence: "While the trial court may exercise wide discretion in determining whether or not proffered evidence shall be admissible, such discretion is subject to appellate review, and the higher court may make an independent determination viewing the record that such discretion was abused") to get you rolling.
5. Start your analysis using the IRAC technique explained below. These letters stand for all the elements necessary for a swift answer.

I—involuntary gagging reflex. This will hit you just as you begin your first sentence. It is a perfectly natural reaction—your epiglottis naturally contracts when your stomach ties itself in a figure-eight knot. Don't worry—this feeling subsides completely after a week.

THE IRAC METHOD FOR ACING LAW SCHOOL EXAMS

I: Involuntary Gagging Reflex

R—rapid eye movement. This next stage of the answer flows smoothly from the first. The student's eyes dart rapidly from his blank blue book back to his scratch-paper outline, as he desperately searches for a course of action. Unfortunately, his outline will invariably list, a result of his panic-stricken subconscious, four dignified ways to commit suicide.

R: Rapid Eye Movement

A—assault the proctor. Again this follows naturally from the preceding stage; convinced that he will flunk, resigned to his imminent suicide, the student naturally decides to take someone with him as he goes. Instinctively, he will attack the closest perpetrator of his misery, the proctor. (Professors know more than to hang around when tests are handed out; they will make a cameo appearance to "answer questions" late in the test after they know the students' initial blind rage has subsided.)

A: Assault the Proctor

C—copy from your neighbors. Having successfully cold-cocked the proctor, our plucky student is now free to avail himself of the wealth of information surrounding him in other students' blue books. Through adept "Iranian Test-Taking" he is able, by comparing and contrasting different answers, to come up with a flawless synthesis that combines all of the best features of the other students' efforts. Test-taking etiquette requires that you start to copy from the student to your right unless his or her answer is up to par, in which case you are free to roam.

C: Copy from Student to Your Right

6. Leave yourself enough TIME. *Never* get tied down answering one question. The other two are just as important, and a heavy Civil Procedure question is *not* completely answered by: "O my God, I spent all of my time on the other two questions, please have mercy. I'll do anything—I swear. O Jesusgivemeabreakplease. I studiedsohardandIjustdon'thaveenough

TIME."

And remember, you are also going to need time to correct your answers, which are blatantly off-the-wall and 100% wrong (something you will discover only as you write your last sentence); time to decipher and copy other students' exams; and time to Scotch-tape large bills inside your blue book.

CHAPTER 8
MURDERER'S ROW
A Guide to Your First-year Courses

When the chill breath of fall cools the air, and it's finally time to retire the zinc oxide, mashie niblicks, and rainbow zorries in favor of pullover sweaters, textbooks, and black rubber G-strings, what young heart does not quicken with the anticipation of new chums, intriguing intellectual challenges, and the invigorating give-and-take of academic banter which the new school year brings? Yours, baby, and don't you forget it. If you wonder why you are experiencing that certain sinking feeling usually associated with Tex-Mex salsa entrees, look no further. We've isolated all of the virulent ingredients contributing to your dolorous condition and are presenting them here for your further enlightenment. They are: your classmates, your professors, and your courses.

While the first two obstacles are human (even if not readily identifiable as such) and therefore manipulable, the last one is etched in bronze. During your first year at Law School you will be presented with the following Beggar's Banquet of a curriculum: Torts, Contracts, Civil Procedure, Property, Criminal Law, and Legal Writing and Research. (This first-year "Dirty Half-Dozen" is augmented by Moot Court at some schools, Constitutional Law at others, and Plea-Copping at certain institutions which rely heavily on matchbook covers for enrollment.) So sharpen your incisors and savor this sampling of your Masochist's Menu. We have highlighted those concepts which have proved to be either extremely important or highly irrelevant.

☐ CRIMINAL LAW AND PROCEDURE

This course explores the constitutional rights guaranteed to an accused before and after custodial arrest. (Note: "custodial arrest" does not mean that you have been arrested by a janitor, although it would be safer that way. It means that you are completely surrounded by the boys in blue, and any sudden movement on your part could result in a sudden case of fatality.) The Exclusionary Rule is discussed, along with such rights as

- ☐ the right to competent counsel (6th Amendment),
- ☐ the right against self-incrimination (5th Amendment), and
- ☐ the right to be free from balding insurance salesmen (16th Amendment).

We have worked hard to put together the following highlights from Criminal Procedure. Memorize them, and then wow your professor with your extensive knowledge of esoterica. You will be cordially asked to leave the class, and you can get on with your plan of making huge bucks as a talk-show host.

Miranda Warning

When the police arrest a miscreant, they must read him his "Miranda Warning" or any subsequent confession will be suppressed, or at least mocked mercilessly in court. Memorize this warning. If the Los Angeles Police can do it, you can, too (although they have been caught using crib sheets, and one lieutenant we know frequently writes it out on his wrist).

1. You have the right to remain silent.
2. You have the right not to be forced to sit repeatedly on a whoopee cushion.
3. You must be told that anything you say may be used to create the theme for a new sit-com of questionable taste, and will probably star an ape, a blonde, or a midget.
4. You may not be forced to wear a Groucho Marx disguise at a pre-indictment lineup without being given some appropriate one-lines.
5. The police may not stage a mock Friars' Roast where one of the officers plays Milton Berle for the sole purpose of humiliating you in front of your cleaning lady.
6. You may not be denied access to your mantra for longer than six hours at a time.
7. Police may not refer to you disdainfully as "Sherman" or "Bernie," unless that is your real name.
8. The police may not lock you in your apartment with your mother-in-law for over three hours without supplying you with a firearm.

Cruel and Unusual Punishment

The following actions have been found to violate the 8th Amendment right against cruel and unusual punishment. There is no hard and fast definition of cruel and unusual punishment, primarily because one man's idea of torture is another man's idea of a great weekend, so the courts have historically contemplated what consititutes cruel and unusual punishment on a case-by-case basis. Following are some examples of police activities that were found to violate the 8th Amendment:

1. Police forced defendant to listen to all of Barry Manilow's greatest hits over a nine-hour period, despite repeated pleas of guilt.
2. Defendant, over his strenuous objections, was force-fed an entire Enchilada Gyro with extra

onions from Steve's House of Souvlaki on Bleecker Street.
3. Defendant was held down bodily by one officer, while the other read out loud selected passages from the *National Geographic* article "Our Friend the Three-Toed Ugandan Desert Newt."
4. Defendant, over his objections, was coerced into attending a cocktail party populated only by CPAs and law students, and was forced to mingle against his will for two hours.
5. Due to a malicious police roadblock, defendant was willfully trapped for 72 hours in Bayonne, New Jersey.
6. Police dressed defendant in a light-blue polyester leisure suit with a Western tie and then took numerous Polaroids without giving defendant a chance to freshen up.

☐ **CONTRACTS**

This course deals with the concepts of offer, acceptance, and consideration, with emphasis on how to avoid them in a pinch. The intricacies of contracts can make it the most maddening course you will take in law school. But one day, as if by magic, all of a sudden, the pieces all fall into place, and merge into elegant simplicity. This usually occurs sometime after your 67th birthday.

You will spend the majority of your Contracts study time trying to discover exactly *when* and *where* the parties stop fooling around and the completed agreement actually becomes a binding contract. (Hint: It usually occurs after 4:00 p.m., just outside of Great Neck.) Once you learn to recognize the formation of a contract, the rest is easy. Because as soon as the contract is formed, one or both parties will breach it, and a free-for-all ensues, during which everyone gets screwed and the lawyers make a lot of money. Now that you understand the basics, we're free to concentrate on some of the flashier doctrines in contracts with an emphasis on those particularly irrelevant, esoteric areas.

Mailbox Rule
This rule was initiated when Judge Learned Hand won a trip to Hawaii in a "Name That Tune" contest. To collect, he had to accept his prize before June 10th. To save money, he mailed a letter on May 8th instead of calling. But the letter arrived June 12th, and the DJ refused to give him the prize. In the subsequent lawsuit, Hand ruled that an acceptance by mail is complete upon *dispatch*, not *receipt*, unless it is mailed from Toledo, Ohio, in which case it is ignored altogether. The rule becomes complicated when the offeree sends a subsequent rejection, which gives the offeror leeway in deciding whether to accept the rejection. But this is simplified by having the rejection delivered personally by a six-foot-five-inch Samoan, in which case the offeror gracefully accepts the rejection and says, "Oh well, perhaps some other time."

Statute of Frauds
The Statute of Frauds (as distinguished from the "Statue of Frauds,"

which is a marble sculpture just outside San Clemente depicting Nixon, Kissinger, and Erlichman at work planning various unspeakable actions) requires that every contract contemplating performance exceeding one year must be in writing, except contracts between Hollywood producers.

Certain other exceptions exist; for example, written contracts aren't required in major heroin deals or agreements to commit arson for profit, but legal authorities suggest something in writing even in these situations, "just to be on the safe side."

Parol Evidence

Once a contract has been reduced to writing consistent with the Statute of Frauds, it is accorded all of the respect that the law has for the sanctity of the written word. Which is to say, it is treated as a total joke; and any evidence that either side can dredge up is admissible to prove that when the writing occurred, both parties were "only kidding." The hardest thing about this doctrine is remembering to leave off the "e" from "parol" when taking a test after you've been up all night on amphetamines.

When in Doubt, Diagram

Frequently, lawyers are presented with fact patterns that are so complex that it is practically impossible to keep the parties and actions straight without using your fingers. Since this method tends to draw attention to you in trial, and can result in remarks from the judge like "Is the widdle plaintiff's counsel-poo having twubble remembering his widdle casey-wasey?" (a question which tends to lower your credibility in the jury's eyes), it is a good idea to cultivate other techniques of sorting out such Gordian knots of facts and issues. After many moons, a favorite trick has emerged as the preferred method of keeping track of the action: diagramming.

Let us take the following fact pattern from a recent case:

Lucinda promises Jon that she will deliver 30 pounds of pickled herring to him to repay him for the terrific mink leisure suit he got for her wholesale. Cooch promises Jon that he will deliver the herring, if Lucinda fails to do so. He then promptly moves to Tahiti, where he stays for the rest of his life.

Jon then assigns his right to the herring to Little Bobby Vegas in return for Bobby's promise not to play his electric guitar at 4:00 a.m., and not to play "New York, New York" ever again.* Bob demands security, and Lucinda pledges her 64-piece set of Fiesta ware. Jon is elated. He then gives Lucie some brand-new rabbit-fur elbow pads. In return, he asks her

*See also "Third-party beneficiaries," p. 69.

to give Richard, whom he owes a favor, her favorite Kat-Klok (the pink one). She reluctantly agrees. Then she promptly leaves for Mykonos, telling Isabella to pay off her debts. Isabella agrees, although she has no idea what the hell Lucie is talking about. This is all very confusing until we sort the parties out, identifying each with a well-accepted, unambiguous term of art and then diagram. Watch how this seemingly imposing fact pattern, once diagrammed, becomes elegantly simple.

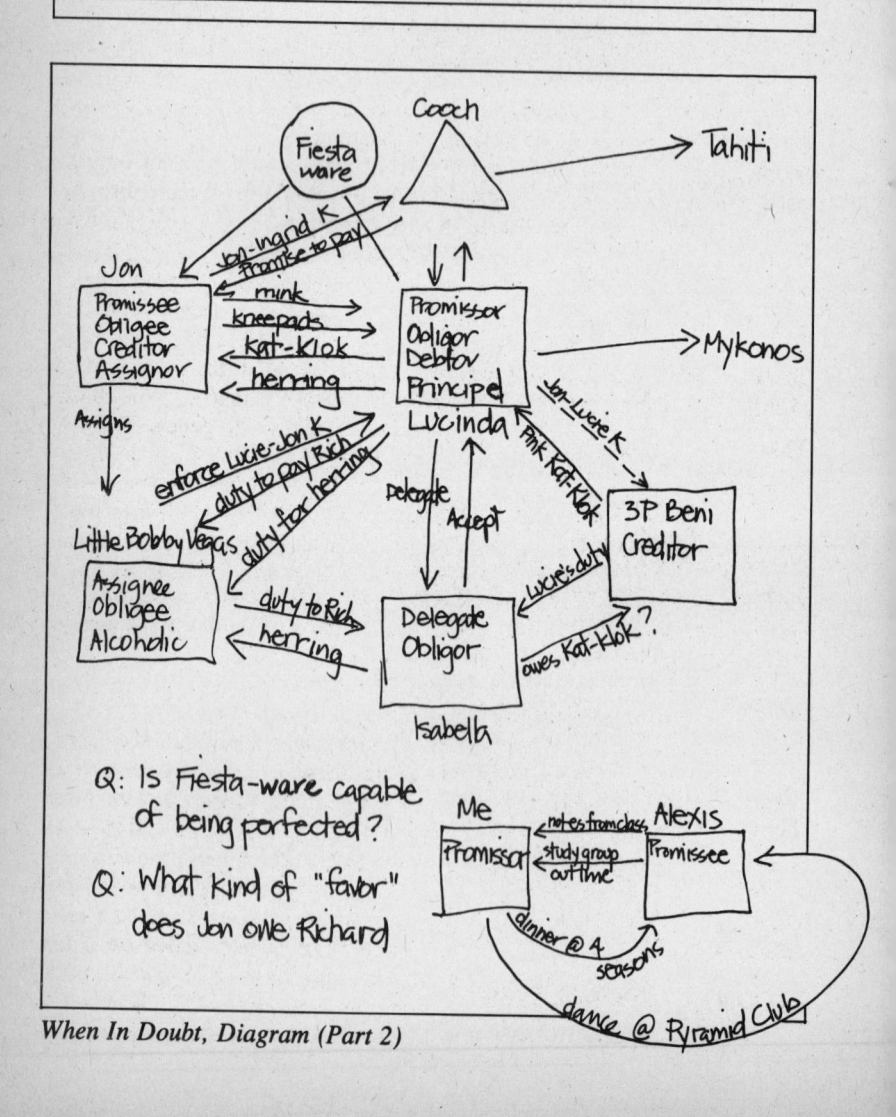

When In Doubt, Diagram (Part 2)

Assignment and Delegation

These will come hopping blithely out of the back of the book and into your final. Just remember that when the promissee assigns, the assignee gets an assignment of the assignor's rights and a delegation of his duties, which makes him both the obligee and obligor of the promissor, who may delegate to anyone he wants, as long as Phyllis Diller is not involved. A delegation occurs when a bunch of delegates (who are all people you never heard of and never voted for) convene and nominate some candidate who makes you puke. Both assignment and delegation should be avoided at all costs, unless you're trying to stick your roommate with your blind date, in which case you will definitely want to invoke both doctrines.

Third-party Beneficiaries

These people are not parties to the contract, but they do benefit from it. Their rights vest as soon as they discover the contract and assent. For example, you promise your roommate, Little Bobby Vegas, a year's supply of pizza if he promises to refrain from playing his electric guitar in your other roommate's shower at 4:00 a.m., and promises to never play "Stairway to Heaven" again as long as he lives. Your roommate is the third-party beneficiary of the Vegas contract, and his rights vest as soon as he finds out about it and kisses your feet repeatedly, weeping in gratitude.

☐ CONSTITUTIONAL LAW

This course is usually a relief to law students because they suddenly find themselves back in what seems like a college American History/Political Science class. They can sit back and watch with amusement as the Supreme Court fabricates its niche in the legislative arena, and using verbal legerdemain, promulgates outlandish interpretations and "doctrines" ostensibly based on the Constitution.

Their amusement soon turns to horror, however, when it becomes obvious that they will not only be expected to suspend their disbelief for an entire year, they will also have to *apply* these linguistic fabrications as if they were ironclad statutes.

Phrases like "national economic effect," "rational basis," and "substantially related to an important government objective," the basic filler which every decent Poli-Sci major used to flesh a three-page paper out to a five-pager without adding any substantive meaning, now constitute the very concepts that can mean the difference between an A or an F. Two of the more important Constitutional concepts you should know are as follows.

Commerce Clause

Everything is based on the Commerce Clause, primarily because in 1849 the court librarian lost the other parts of the Consitution and was too embarrassed to tell anyone about it, so he printed the Commerce Clause over and over. As a result, four generations of justices relied on it for everything from child labor to milk pasteurizing, following Marshall's maxim, "Any clause in a pinch."

Strict Scrutiny

If a fundamental right is involved, or if the defendant is in a suspect class, the court will apply "strict scrutiny" to determine whether the means used are *"substantially related"* to a *"compelling state interest."* (Be still, my beating heart.) It is felt that certain rights and certain classes of people deserve more protection than others. Fundamental rights include the right to fall asleep during Ingmar Bergman movies, the right to make fun of people who own Winnebagos, and the right to refuse to eat liver no matter how it's cooked.

There are seveal suspect classes, but it is universally agreed that the most suspect are maître d's, female impersonators, people who eat tofu, and the Harvard Class of 1975.

☐ CIVIL PROCEDURE

In this course, you will be taught the intricate, elegant procedure which enables an attorney to bring amorphous, abstract, substantive rights to a tangible and just resolution. In other words, how, using civil procedure, two competent attorneys can transform their clients' claims into a complete travesty.

In Civil Procedure you are taught how to bring a case to trial, how to appeal a case you've lost, and how to dress when you are jailed for contempt of court. At good law schools, you will also be taught 200 ingratiating and obsequious phrases to use in front of a judge. Some lawyers have won many cases using this technique alone without having to resort to civil procedure; it saves tremendously on paperwork.

Following are some of the more important concepts you will learn in Civil Procedure.

Garnishee

In *Harris* v. *Balk*, the court established that a plaintiff could attach a debt owed by a third party to a defendant to establish jurisdiction. More important, it implied in dictum that grown men could now use the word "garnishee" as a verb. So instead of saying "I hereby garnish your debt," which is silly enough on its own, lawyers now say "I hereby garnishee your debt," without cracking a smile. The court tried to amend this faux pas by ruling in a subsequent case that garnisheeing could *not* be done to confer jurisdiction, but it was too late—by then lawyers were garnisheeing for the fun of it.

Joinder

Proper joinder of parties is critical to the success of a lawsuit. Generally speaking, if you are a corporate lawyer it is a good idea to join the Republican Party; personal injury lawyers should become democrats, and entertainment lawyers should become Jewish.

The court will employ various criteria to determine whether the parties are "necessary" or "indespensable." As a general rule of thumb, parties thrown by Andy Warhol are necessary, but parties thrown by Jackie O., or any royalty, are indispensable.

Claims will be joined if there is a "common nucleus of operative fact." Again, the courts will employ common sense in making this determination (since it is easier than doing research).

For example, joinder was denied when it was found that the only thing the parties had in common was their desire to meet Ethel Mertz on the *I Love Lucy* show and that they thought Robert Morley's performance in *African Queen* could have been stronger.

Similarly, the court refused to join two claims when it was pointed out that the claims shared no similarities other than the fact that they both used the word "herein" 147 times, contained 12 misspellings, and had ketchup stains on the back.

In denying joinder, the court sagely concluded, "We cannot allow joinder where the only common nucleus of operative fact that we can find is that the attorneys are both bozos."

The so-called "Bozo Test" remains the standard today, at least in federal courts.

Subject Matter Jurisdiction

An attorney must show a court that it possesses subject matter jurisdiction over the claim before the court will entertain the controversy. Courts can't entertain everything—in fact, some critics maintain that judges do far too much entertaining already, and suggest that they stay home and read once in a while instead of going out break-dancing at the Mudd Club every night.

Federal courts require diversity of citizenship, among other things, before they will listen to a plaintiff. To attain diversity of citizenship, both the plaintiff and the defendant must have at least one parent who is not American (preferably French), must have vacationed extensively in Europe, and must speak at least one foreign language, or be able to fake it at cocktail parties. The requirement guarantees that only genteel cosmopolitan people will appear before federal court.

Class Action

This is an attempt by the courts "to bring a little style back into litigation." The subject matter must be appropriate (for example, any case in which Katharine Hepburn is plaintiff is a class action), and attorneys are requested to wear creative black tie to court. Popular in the '70s, the class action is now being tightened up by the Supreme Court, partly to cut down on the hors d'oeuvre catering costs, and partly because "we were starting to see too many velveteen tuxedos in your basic station wagon colors."

☐ TORTS

Torts is fun. In torts we learn that anything is possible, and that there is always somebody to blame (usually a blender company). In short, we learn proximate cause. We find that starting a cable car too fast results in nymphomania, that failing to put a warning on the microwave oven results in a lady putting her poodle in there to dry, and in the following now-famous case, the court held that art appreciation leads naturally and inevitably to nuclear war.

Facts

At approximately 2:30 p.m., the Met unveiled a Modigliani which had been missing for 12 years, and which everyone believed stolen until it was discovered quite accidentally by the head art curator, who stumbled across it hanging over the mantelpiece in his living room. ("Boy, was my face red," he cheerfully admitted.) Upon seeing it, a fine arts professor from Columbia fell into a histrionic swoon which borrowed heavily from the death scene in *Carmen* but was impressive enough in its own right to earn light applause from the other art patrons gathered around the painting.

In the process, however, he inadvertently stepped on the tail of a particularly vicious dog. The dog, who was severely myopic, promptly sank his teeth into the ankle of a dark, furtive figure who had been lurking on the outskirts of the crowd fondling the Rodins. The dark, furtive figure immediately let out a shriek and then accurately drop-kicked the dog 35 yards across the museum, where the punted pooch crash-landed on the buffet counter of the cafeteria, scattering Swedish meatballs at high velocity. Several of the meatballs struck dining patrons, someone yelled, "Food fight!" and the battle was on, with NATO countries controlling the pasta section while the Eastern Bloc countries operated from the cold-cuts counter.

A reporter from the *New York Post*, trapped in the melee, quickly donned his camouflage fatigues and, safely disguised as a large Jell-O dessert, crawled to a phone and made his report. Within hours the story was out. With characteristic journalistic restraint, the *Post* headlined the front-page article, "U.S. and Russia at WAR!! WAR! WAR! Do you hear me? WAR!"

A KGB agent assigned to Rudy's 53rd Street newsstand, alarmed by the headline, leaped into action and immediately shortwaved the Kremlin as soon as he had finished playing Wingo and done the crossword puzzle. Upon hearing the bad news of impending global destruction, the Soviet Premier, who had been having a lousy week as it was, called President Reagan on the hot line. "Ron," he said, "I don't want to sound testy, but have you launched several thousand ICBMs? Because I've got about 3,000 SSTs here ready to ruin your whole weekend if you have. You had to pick a week like this, when I have such headaches?" Reagan assured the Soviet lead that he had no plans for a nuclear attack until after his reelection. "Nancy hasn't finished decorating yet, for gosh sakes!" he chided. Reassured that Reagan had not attacked yet, the Soviet Premier breathed a sigh of relief and promptly launched all 3,000 Russian missiles.

It is also in Torts that you will be introduced to the most popular, if predictably bland character in jurisprudence: the Reasonable Man. Since he rarely makes public appearances, he remains, for all of his exposure, somewhat of an enigma to all but his closest friends. Imagine our surprise and good luck, then, to run across this revealing ad in the personal Classifieds of *Spanking Time*, June issue:

PERSONAL CLASSIFIED

The Reasonable Man

SWM, 35, Virgo, fun-loving but sensible, medium height, average weight, looks, and intelligence. Seeking compatible, reasonable woman (pref. Aquarius) to hold up to the highest standard of care. I'm tired of the bar scene, of flashy attractive nuisances, of hidden ultrahazardous conditions.

Are you fed up with always assuming the risk? Don't you wish you could reasonably rely on someone who will be aware of your special sensitivities, who appreciates the child in you as well as the adult? Someone who won't shock you with extreme and outrageous conduct? Someone who will listen to what you say, and understand, without reading a lot of hidden meanings into it? A man who says what he means and means what he says? Well, here I am. This is your last clear chance!

I enjoy food and drink, but in moderation. I don't believe you have to go beyond reasonable expectations just to have a good time. No drugs—I get high on life (not too high—just high enough). I believe life is a journey—and as long as we go at the proper speed and obey all the signs, it can be beautiful. Will you share my journey? R.M., P.O. Box 102. (Please include photo with letter. No drag queens or fems, please.)

☐ **PROPERTY**

Most of the legal principles which comprise property originated over three centuries ago in what became Europe during a particularly enlightened period called the Dark Ages—and they are as logical and equitable today as when they were first promulgated.

You may ask, "What is the value of studying feudal principals edicted by Anglo-Saxon barbarians for the express purpose of oppressing the serfs, taxing their underwear off, and assuring that they would never own property?" If you are asking this, you obviously have never rented an apartment in New York.

At first, these arcane, convoluted

"doctrines" may strike you as slightly irrelevant to a law student in the 20th century. However, after you gain a more complete and incisive comprehension of them, it will dawn on you — they are *totally* irrelevant. Your professor will tell you as much, but will then add that you will be responsible for all of them on the test anyway. Which gives them a big boost, relevancewise.

Normally, the most ancient and anachronistic concept you will face in Property will be the professor. (For a complete discussion of this ancient species, see *Chapter 10*.) And your biggest problem in Property will be staying awake in class without using artificial stimulants. In fact, medical studies have found that it is impossible to distinguish between a student in a coma and a student in Property. The only difference seems to be that it is possible to come out of a coma within a few days or weeks, whereas Property lasts for an entire year. A follow-up study conducted years later on practicing attorneys found that 86% of them could be plunged involuntarily into a deep trancelike state simply by hearing the word "Blackacre."

We will not discuss here the ancient doctrines such as the Statute of Queen Anne, the Rule of Shelley's Case, Dumpor's Case, the Doctrine of Worthier Title, because we don't want to deprive your professor of the joy of looking out on a sea of grimacing faces. However, we will cover some of the more incredible modern concepts, in hope of helping you avoid that feeling of vertigo which will become so distressingly familiar in law school.

Seisin

This is an ancient ritual that was performed to pass ownership of the "bundle of rights" from the property seller to the buyer. (These rights were represented by a bundle of small sticks, or "faggots" as they were called in those days — sellers preferred the bundle of sticks, as the faggots were harder to round up, complained a lot, and always argued over who got to play Joan Crawford.) Typically, the owner would draw a circle in the ground with a stick, then he would draw the dimensions of the property on the buyer's forehead, using fingerpaints. The buyer would then remove his or her shirt and do the Boogaloo, the Frug, or the Sassy-Bump, depending on the value of the property, until his/her shoes were completely covered with dirt, thus symbolically accepting the seisin. For life estates, a shortened modified ritual was followed, with the buyer gatoring while the seller did an imitation of Bebe Rebozo eating a taco.

Recording Statutes

The tough part here is telling the difference between a notice and a race-notice statute. Some scholars recommend the widely accepted coin toss, but an emerging school favors counting the words in the statute: If there are more than 37 words, it is a race-notice statute.

A race-notice statute requires that in addition to recording, the new owner must compete in a local potato-bag race and place at least third. She need not win one of those troll dolls with shag-pile fuchsia hair, but if she does, she is safe even from a Bona Fide Purchaser. Most jurisdictions will accept a buyer recording with the county clerk, although they vastly prefer it if she can record with Martha and the Vandellas.

Future Interests
This chapter of Property derives its name from the fact that when students are confronted by it, they immediately develop future interests in fields other than law. But as with other seemingly incomprehensible areas of law, once you learn to *identify* the Property interest, the rest is easy.

On the Property exam, you will read about someone who deeds (or wills) his property to about 17 different people, demanding that each of them commit various humiliating acts to hold on to his or her piece. Look at the language. If it says, "To Herbie, *as long as* he does not wear girls' dresses," it is a Fee Simple Determinable. If it says, "To Herbie, *on condition that* he avoids doing Bette Davis imitations," it is Fee Simple subject to a Condition Subsequent. If it says, "To Herbie and his heirs, *but if* the property is *ever* used for a drag cabaret, then to the Ku Klux Klan," then it is a Fee Simple Subject to an Executory Limitation, and you can kiss your grade goodbye, because the question is about the Rule Against Perpetuities, your prof is a sadist, and you're going to flunk. In such a case, the traditional coin toss is your best bet. Chin up! There's always the chance that your tears will disguise your answer by making the ink run.

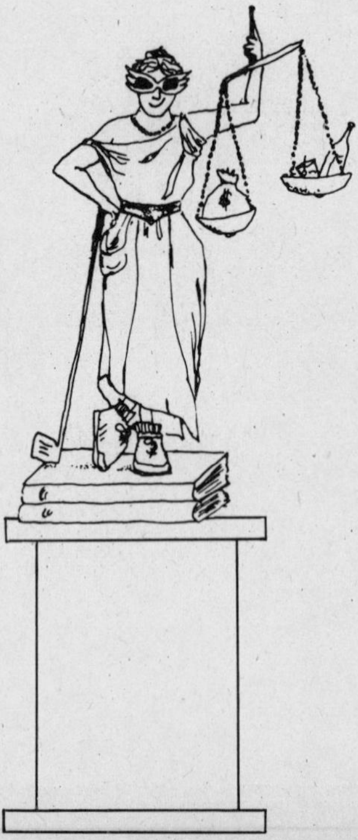

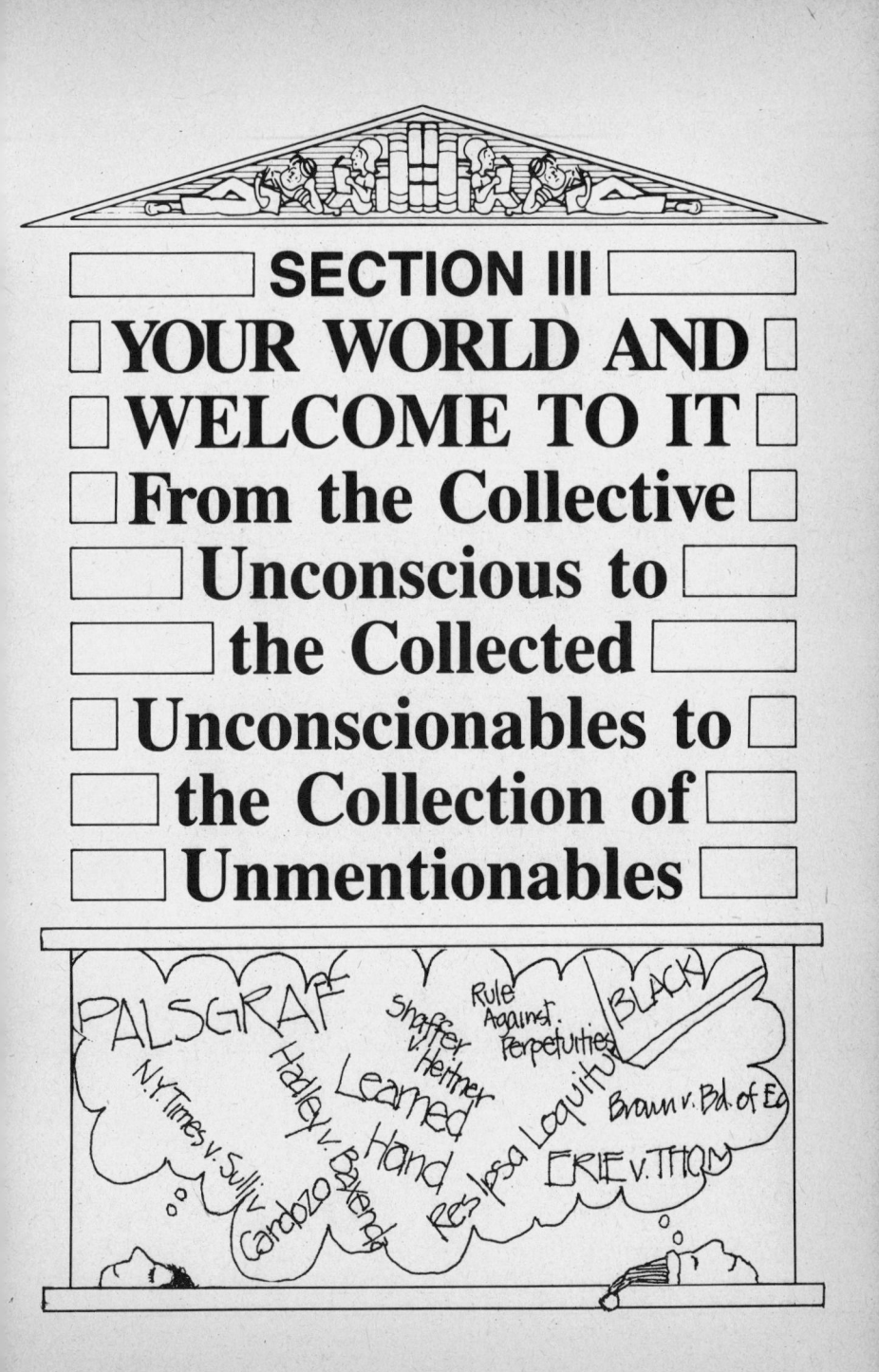

SECTION III
YOUR WORLD AND WELCOME TO IT
From the Collective Unconscious to the Collected Unconscionables to the Collection of Unmentionables

HOW LAWS ARE MADE
Contestant Pat Ward wins his case when Justice O'Connor tips the majority with her impressive recall of "Leave it to Beaver" trivia—and new law is made!

CHAPTER 9
THE COLLECTIVE UNCONSCIOUS
What Every Law Student Must Know

☐ SIGNIFICANT CASES AND CONCEPTS

From the time that you enter law school until you die, when hobnobbing with legal colleagues, you will be expected—if not required—to chuckle, nod knowingly, or meaningfully raise your eyebrow at the mention of one of a number of significant cases, even long after you have forgotten their importance, assuming you ever knew it in the first place. (Note: The following list is a bare *minimum*. Obviously, the more case names, terms of the art and concepts you can refer to, the greater your panache in any law school discussion, courtroom battle, or, more important, cocktail party.)

PENNOYER v. NEFF 18 U.S.C. 634

This case is significant only because it is the first jurisdiction case that law students everywhere encounter in Civil Procedure. No one is sure about exactly what happened in this case, including your Civil Procedure professor, but he'll spend two weeks on the case, anyway.

HADLEY v. BAXENDALE 115 Cal. App. 362

This Contracts case holds that the breacher is liable to the injured party for foreseeable damages, frequently referred to as consequential or *Hadley* v. *Baxendale* damages. Law partners who wish to have unlisted phone numbers invariably list this name in the phone book—Baxendale, Hadley V. This is considered an enormously cute thing to do. The practice started in Houston, Texas, and has spread nationwide while expanding its repertoire to include names of other cases, but Baxendale is still the original laff riot.

☐ 79

PALSGRAF V. LONG ISLAND RAILROAD 36 N.Y. App. Div. 1492

This case is BIG. Bigger than big. In this case, Moses comes down from the mountain in the form of Justices Cardozo and Andrews, carrying the tablets with the long-awaited definition of "proximate cause" etched in stone for the wandering generations of tort lawyers, who will spend the next 100 years trying to refine, define, and divine what, exactly, the two were talking about.

You can wow your friends with this trivia. The facts are as follows: A man with a mysterious package is helped onto a train by a railroad employee. In the process, the embarking passenger drops the package (of explosives), which explodes, causing a scale on the far end of the platform to fall and hit Mrs. Palsgraf—guess where it hit her? Your professor would rather not talk about this.

MARBURY V. MADISON 1 U.S.C. 14

In this case, the Supreme Court (under Justice Marshall, to give credit where it is due) made its big move. Marshall asserted that while the Supreme Court does not have the power to legislate under the Constitution, it does have the power to review the constitutionality of legislation passed by Congress, even though there is no express provision to that effect. This solipsism confused Congress so completely that it was another 50 years before they realized that they had been had, and by then it was too late. The Supreme Court, except for a brief, nervous period in which F.D.R. was going to fire all nine Justices, has been merrily "interpreting" (i.e., legislating) ever since.

UNITED STATES V. NIXON 418 U.S. 683

In this case, a small-time gangster found out, much to his shock and chagrin, that he was not above the law. He refused to comply with a subpoena duces tecum properly requesting the tapes of his private conversations with fellow thugs in which he discussed rub-outs, payoffs, and various obstructions of justice. He asserted in his brief, "I am the President. P-R-E-S-I-D-E-N-T. Do you hear me? I don't do *anything* I don't want to. And that includes obeying the law."

In the Court's opinion, the justices noted, with deference, that Nixon *was* indeed President, and that while a lot of people had paid a lot of money to get him in there and it was slightly unfair to deprive them of their boy after all that cash, he was being *very* naughty, and that the "I am the President" button stapled to his brief did not qualify for a claim of Executive Privilege. They then pointed out that this time he was dealing with adults, and had better hand over the tapes.

So Honest John Sirica was treated to an in-camera session with the tapes of the highest officials of the country making executive governmental policy decisions which would guide the United States for the next four years. Unfortunately, it was not the sweeping epic he had hoped for—just some small-time thugs trying to play big-time gangsters by using dirty grownup words.

BLACKACRE

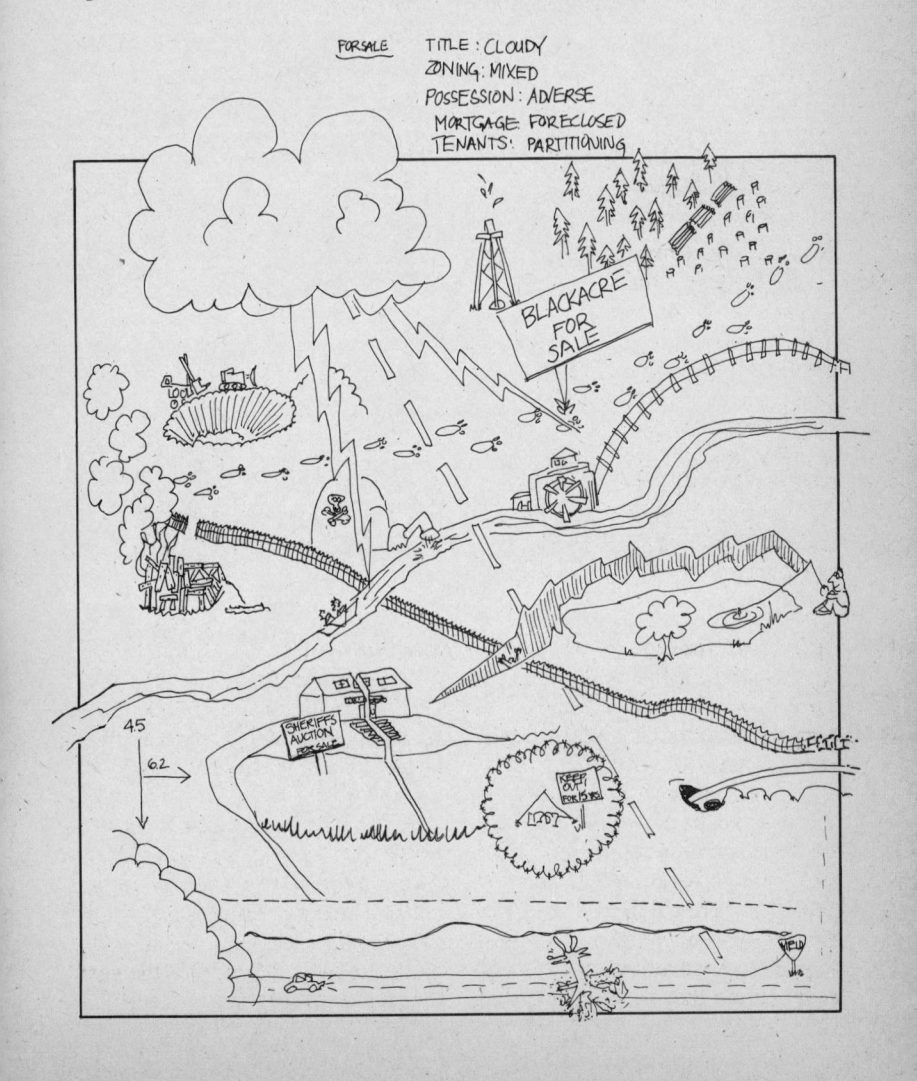

This is the most bought, sold, mortgaged, liened, zoned, inherited, built upon, torn-down, carved-up, severed, fenced-in, driven-over, flown-over, squatted-on, drilled, milled, and filled, constructed, destructed, partitioned, rented, leased, put-up-as-collateral, foreclosed, deeded, recorded, infringed-upon, covenanted, equitable-servituded, touched and concerned piece of property in the world, and possibly the known universe. It's a wonder there is anything left. Fortunately, some of the burden is shared by Whiteacre and Greenacre, but the old workhorse will always be Blackacre.

THE RULE AGAINST PERPETUITIES

When you hear this common law doctrine mentioned, groan out loud and shake your head, then chuckle in disbelief. Everyone else will be doing the same. This is the Rubik's Cube of the law: if you think you understand it, you're just kidding yourself. But relax—a lawyer cannot be sued for malpractice for screwing up this concept.

NEW YORK TIMES V. SULLIVAN 361 V.S. 1406

The Supreme Court held in this case that where the plaintiff in a defamation action is a public figure and the defendant is a media defendant (newspapers, etc.), the plaintiff has to prove actual malice in addition to the prima facie case. Legalese being what it is, "actual malice" predictably has nothing to do with real malice. It means that the newspaper published a falsehood knowingly or with reckless disregard for its truth or falsity.

This is why the *Daily Blatt* can get away with stories like "Burt Reynolds—I Was the Father of My Sister's Only Brother"... they actually believe it.

ERIE V. THOMPKINS 21 U.S. 431

The Supreme Court held in this case that a federal district court has to apply the substantive law of the state in which it sits. This has been interpreted by subsequent cases to mean "Federal courts will apply the substantive law of the state—if they're in the mood." For this reason, most good attorneys will check a district court judge's horoscope before removing a case from state court to federal court.

☐ SMOOTH JUDGES AND WHY WE LIKE THEM

Once upon a time, a judge who had run out of relevant things to say about the case in his opinion disgressed into musings on the role of magistrates: "Law is a shimmering canvas upon which each justice, employing all of his skill and wisdom, seeks to interpret the dim outlines of truth into a complete image of harmony and beauty, capable of elevating the spirit of mankind."

If we forgive the florid phrase-monger his metaphor (and there is no reason we should), the next question is: "How, among the rhetorical Rembrandts, do I tell the Picassos from the Leroy Niemans? I don't know enough about law to tell a brilliantly trenchant, exquisitely sculpted opinion from one that is merely incomprehensible."

The answer is simple—there are some judges who can do no wrong, and as for the others, don't worry. Your professor will always let you know what he thinks of an opinion if you listen carefully to his tone. A statement like "This is the worst collection of retrograde swamp gas I've ever waded through" means he's not impressed.

Here, then, is a nonexhaustive list of the Picassos of Prose, the Leonardos of Logic, the Giacomettis of Jurisprudence. They constitute the All-Pro team of Juridical Giants. In other words, if one of these limners of *lex scripta* signed the opinion, it is a masterpiece. So you love it. Even if it reads like Timothy Leary on Quaaludes.

Name	Nominated by	Years served
John Jay	Washington	1789–1795
John Marshall	Adams	1801–1835
Oliver W. Holmes	T. Roosevelt	1902–1932
Louis Brandeis	Wilson	1916–1939
Benjamin Cardozo	Hoover	1932–1938
Hugo Black	F. Roosevelt	1937–1971
Felix Frankfurter	F. Roosevelt	1939–1962
William O. Douglas	F. Roosevelt	1939–1975
Earl Warren	Eisenhower	1953–1969

Of course it is practically de rigueur to disagree over the decisions of the more recent all-star choices (i.e., since Hoover) shown above, as it implies that you have profound historical and philosophical depth which enables you to dismiss certain justices as petty and give the nod to others, whose families, no doubt, are grateful for your vote of confidence.

There are, of course, other terrific (non-Supreme) judges with whom the freshman pseudo-cognoscente should be on a first-name basis. There is the terrible trio of Learned Hand, Minor Wisdom, and Barefoot Saunders. Then there are the "cute name" judges, Henry J. Friendly, E. Grady Jolly, Proctor Hug, James Moody, Thomas A. Wiseman, Eugene and Niel F. Lynch, Joseph Hatchett, Harry T. Lemmon, and, of course, Justice William W. Justice. Armed with this trivia, you'll leave 'em in stitches at the next law school wine and cheese party.

☐ NEANDERTHAL LAWS (STATUTES AND RULINGS) THAT ARE STILL ON THE BOOKS

Nothing has changed in law administration since Moses. The divinely inspired code is handed down to a wise man with an impressive speaking voice and a robe, who interprets the code and adds a few rules of his own. Then the huddled masses, impressed by the sagacity and moral correctness of the various edicts, immediately set about violating every one of them. Lawyers both prosecute and defend these offenders, depending on who hires them, and get rich in the process.

But above all these mortal shenanigans there is the law of the land, stern, silent, wise, and just. Law is the conscience and soul of society. The legislators and judges are the brains, lawyers are the strong hands, the police are... what the hell is this, an essay on law or a damn biology lesson?

Getting back to the point, laws are written by legislators, intelligent, moral, and impartial men and women who, in their search for an ideal society, are above the petty grasp of special interest groups—unless, of course, the touted legislation will benefit the community at large by adding a swimming pool and tennis court to the senator's backyard (via a donation from a grateful lobbyist). Everyone likes driving through neighborhoods with swimming pools and tennis courts —they are aesthetically very pleasing.

The following laws, statutes, and rulings have been, or are still, on the books in the states indicated. They represent but a small sampling of the collective wisdom of our courts and legislatures.*

*For a more extensive and well-researched compilation of laws, see Dick Hyman, *The Trenton Pickle Ordinance and Other Bonehead Legislation* (Brattleboro, Vt.: Stephen Greene Press, 1976.)

☐ DUBIOUS DECREES STILL ON THE BOOKS

- The Virginia Code (1930) has a statute outlawing "corrupt practices or bribery by any person other than candidates."

- It is illegal to allow a pet cat to run loose without a taillight in Sterling, Colorado.

- In Idaho, a person must have a permit from the sheriff to buy chicken after dark.

- In Nebraska, a husband is justified in slapping his wife if he can show that it was necessary to do so in order to compel her to go out for the benefit of her health.

- In Massachusetts, it is illegal to put tomatoes in clam chowder.

- A Pennsylvania statute provides protection for husbands: "A husband is not guilty of desertion when his wife rents his room to a boarder and crowds him out of the house."

- In Groton, Connecticut, the law asserts that "any utterances from a man in a bow-tie are not to be credited."

- In Anchorage, Alaska, by statute, "every year all male residents shall

THE COLLECTIVE UNCONSCIOUS □ 85

raise beards from January 5th to the middle of February," when a celebration called the Fur Rendezvous is held.

• A citizen "may not go around imitating animals" in Miami.

• In Washington, D.C. it is forbidden "to exert pressure on a balloon and thereby cause a whistling sound on the streets."

• It is against the law to bite your landlord in Rumford, North Carolina.

• A Belt, Montana, statute forbids the Tango, the Duck Wobble, the Angle Worm Wiggle, and the Kangaroo Glide.

• "All persons who shall be found at any time underneath sidewalks" shall be guilty of disorderly conduct in Florida.

• An Oneida, Tennessee, ordinance forbids anyone to sing the song, "It n't Goin' to Rain No Mo."

• Women in Joliet, Illinois, can be jailed for trying on more than six dresses in a store.

• **A Chicago law forbids eating in a place that is on fire.**

• It is a misdemeanor in Georgia for any citizen to attend church worship on Sunday unless he is equipped with a rifle and it is loaded.

• It is illegal to fish on the Chicago breakwater in pajamas.

• In West Virginia, it is a penal offense to cook sauerkraut or cabbage, as the ensuing odors are public nuisance.

- Hickory, North Carolina, provides that drunken driving means "steering an automobile with motor on or off."
- Pharmacists in Trout Creek, Utah, may not sell gunpowder as a headache cure.
- In Owensboro, Kentucky, it is illegal for a woman to buy a new hat unless her husband tries it on first.
- Kansas law prohibits shooting rabbits from a motorboat.
- It is against the law to get a fish drunk in Oklahoma.
- It is against the law in Washington, D.C., to paint lemons on your car so as to embarrass your auto dealer.
- It is against the law to buy, sell, raise, or give away a parrot in the state of Georgia.

CHAPTER 10
THE PRE-INDICTMENT LINEUP:
Law School's Cast of Characters

Let's start with an upbeat quote from the Princeton student guide, "Welcome to Law School."*

"On registration day, you will look out over a sea of happy faces. Happy, unattractive faces. It will come as a great shock to you that this motley collection of humorless ferrets, this coven of misanthropic nebbishes, this toolbox of Uriah Heeps, this pack of *Homo lupus*, in short, this Petri dish of mono-lobed mutations, is to become your 'brethren.' But it is true. These are your comrades, who will be fighting alongside you in the trenches. And, to a man, they will not hesitate to cut you down from behind whenever they get the chance. Any 'friendship' you may encounter will be grounded purely in self-preservation and will be dropped as soon as it ceases to be advantageous.

"So keep your head up and don't get taken. And remember the sage words of our dean: 'In law school it is important not to fall behind. This is because we eat our wounded. Good luck and have a nice day!'"

This rather cynical assessment of first-year law students suffers from its one-sided point of view. It neglects to point out the attributes of many of the students and instead focuses on what we shall call, for lack of a better word, the truth. In doing so, it tends to lump all law students into a human landfill, thus denying each individual his unique abilities and goals to pursue truth, to pursue grades, and to become a royal pain in the ass in his own right.

As it would be facile and unfair to deny each student-type his own in-depth analysis, we have procured a pictorial chart prepared by the Anthropological Law Professors' Organization (ALPO) which accurately and comprehensively delineates each genus. This prof's-eye view of a representative selection of students in their natural classroom habitat affords a good overview of the species, from individual protective coloring to personal (usually annoying) idiosyncrasies, and captures each in characteristic behavior.

*So Princeton doesn't have a law school—so what? They have Brooke Shields.

87

88 □ YOUR WORLD AND WELCOME TO IT

□ THE STUDENTS: A Bestiary

THE BACK OF THE BUS GANG

ROW 3: *Odd Lots*

ROW 2: *Hot Shots*

ROW 1: *Red-Hots*

ROW 1
Nerdum grindomaximus
Markings: Casebook, hornbook, typed brief, typed outline, book stand, B.O.
Characteristics: Becomes sexually aroused by seeing his grades, which are always good. They ought to be. He outlines the textbooks over the summer and spends 140 hours a week studying.
Adult: Joins 250-attorney firm. Works on single antitrust case for the rest of his life. Has wife and kids, but isn't sure what their names are.
Identifying call: "The Second Circuit decision cited in footnote 17 would appear superficially to support the court's dictum, but upon closer analysis, it can be distinguished on several points."

ROW 1
Spiritum willingus fleshum weak
Markings: No-Doz, incoherent notes.
Characteristics: Earnest but frail. Studies all night, every night, and collapses during the day. Sits in front row, hoping fear and terror will keep her awake—no dice. During final exams, she stays up 104 hours straight, writes 4,000-word answer—all on the first line of her answer book.
Adult: Joins litigation firm, stays up for weeks before trial, sleeps through cross-examination. Disbarred, she becomes a successful businesswoman, and for the first time, gets some sleep.
Identifying call: "What? Oh, *excuse* me. Could you please repeat... well, oh, actually, I'm afraid I'll have to pass."

ROW 1
Studentaeum grandmammus
Markings: Casebook, briefs, children's wedding pictures.
Characteristics: Sits in front row for sound academic reasons: so she can see and hear the professor. Hardworking, but drifts frequently due to preoccupation with her daughter who never calls and never writes.
Adult: Becomes state representative for her wealthy suburb.
Identifying call: "I'm sorry... could you repeat the question a little louder, please?"

92 □ YOUR WORLD AND WELCOME TO IT

ROW 1
Animus politicas sycophantum
Markings: Student facebook, political fundraising handbook.
Characteristics: Knows the name of every student and professor by the second day—they are his future constituency, after all. Overly hearty and ingratiating. Heads student council in the hopes of favorably impressing influential deans.
Adult: Joins DA's office to show his public commitment and to make political contacts. After a year of drunk-driving cases, he builds his war chest and runs for office. He loses.
Identifying call: "As you so astutely noted in this case, Professor Walsh, the issue, as you said, is collateral estoppel."

ROW 2
Agentiam Hollywoodus
Markings: Loud Hawaiian party shirt, wrap-around mirror shades, *Variety* and *Billboard* magazines.
Characteristics: Encyclopedic knowledge of cocaine-case precedents. Casual. Law school is just a temporary inconvenience on his way to becoming Diana Ross's personal manager. Not particularly concerned about grades as long as dad owns ICM.
Adult: Manages several New Wave groups including the Dangerous Debs, Warm Leatherette, and Face Drano. Also, Fleetwood Mac. House in Malibu. Frequent nosebleeds.
Identifying call: "Well, like the court was totally adamant, but the holding is ultimately pretty meaningless, since it's not a California or New York case."

ROW 2
Bombshellus blondorum
Markings: Flawless suntan, smile, eyes, knees, etc. Can stop a speeding train at 30 yards by batting eyelashes.
Characteristics: Separates relevant from irrelevant facts with ease. Relevant facts are what the Beautiful People (and she) are up to this weekend, and law school gossip (which she thrives on hearing and creating). Irrelevant facts are everything else. Not averse to discreet "private tutoring" with good-looking prof.
Adult: Gets a job with a good firm because the senior partner "likes her style." Competent lawyer, but quits to star in movie with Robert Redford, directed by her "good friend" whom she met in Acapulco.
Identifying call: "Well, I'll *try* to brief this case, if you *promise* to be nice to me."

ROW 2
Loco parentus
Markings: Station-wagon keys and finger paint on textbooks, child in diapers, with crayons, on lap.
Characteristics: Chatty, slightly peeved that law school thoughtlessly does not provide cribs or hobby horses in student lounges. Came to school to "get out of the house." Forms study group with other law school moms— it turns into a bridge club.
Adult: After she passes the Bar, word gets around and all the mothers in the neighborhood come to her when their appliances break. She gets results. Becomes consumer advocate with her own radio show.
Identifying call: "The issue in this case is whether defendant is estopped from... *Thomas*! Get that eraser out of your *mouth*!"

ROW 2
Geniusum recalcitrantus
Markings: Blushing cheeks, soft voice, lives at home, neat notes, neat books, neat clothes, neat everything.
Characteristics: Because she is shy and unassuming, and looks like everybody's 15-year-old kid sister, nobody pays any attention to her—until the finals are graded and it is announced that she is number one in the class. She is suddenly deluged with offers to join study groups, come to parties, or "just be friends" by red-hots, who figure she can help them make Law Review. She will politely decline.
Adult: She unobtrusively pursues her career, which very few people follow until, at the age of 37, she is appointed to the highest state court, a feat which amazes everyone—except her. She planned this from the start. New "friends" will make her offers and once again she will politely decline.
Identifying call: "Well, in your hypothesis, the executory gift to the Foundation would be invalid, because it could conceivably vest later than 21 years after a life in being—but I'm assuming here that there is no exception for gift-overs to charities."

THE PRE-INDICTMENT LINEUP □ 97

ROW 3
Minoritorum meritorus
Markings: Periodicals, *Public Interest Law Quarterly* magazine, Tenant Defense Workshop.
Characteristics: Although he got a 3.6 at Harvard and a 49 on his LSAT, he has an irrational suspicion that the professor considers him underqualified and will make every attempt to humiliate him. It's true. He does, and he will. But the prof feels that way about *everybody*, so he shouldn't feel so special.
Adult: After clerking for pro bono and public interest agencies for two summers, he will be lured by a big firm, make a lot of money, then run for office. He will win.
Identifying call: "Perhaps you didn't hear me. I said, I *pass*. When I have something to say about this case, I'll let you know."

ROW 3

Humanitas spiritus

Markings: Pamphlets - "Law and the Disadvantaged," "Poverty Law," "Defending Pro Bono cases."

Characteristics: Very serious and conscientious. Too busy to listen in class because she is writing a habeas corpus brief on behalf of a prisoner. As she is one of the few tolerable women in the class, guys will try to date her, but give up when they discover that she'd rather save the whales than have sex.

Adult: Opens own practice between shuttling from Tenant Defense League to the American Indian Rights workshop. Because of her involvement in local community affairs, she is eventually elected to the City Board of Supervisors.

Identifying call: "Frankly, I'm tired of hearing about 'judicial efficiency' in these cases—when will the court concern itself with *justice*?"

THE PRE-INDICTMENT LINEUP □ 99

ROW 3
Earnestiam cluelessae
Markings: Casebook, canned briefs, six outlines, notes from private tutorial.
Characteristics: This doggedly earnest type never "quite" gets it. He studies 20 hours a day, but is still continually baffled. He sees law as a way of gaining respect and making money, and dreams of the day he can wear a suit and be a "professional"—but why must everything be so *hard* to *understand*? It must have something to do with hand-eye coordination.
Adult: Works for small, mediocre probate firm, but this is still too mentally taxing. So he becomes Vice-President of the United States. Gravy at last.
Identifying call: "Certainly. In this case, the plaintiff was from Ohio... he wasn't? God, I could have *sworn*—what about the defendant? Federal Rules of Interpleader? No, I don't know the code number. Sorry."

ROW 3
Radicalorum
bourgeoisis
Markings: Jesus hair, bead necklace, no shirt, Earth shoes. "Spartacist" newspaper.
Characteristics: Has been a militant hippie ever since Exeter. Ready for a confrontation with any authority figure including the school janitor. Relates heavily to the sexism, racism, and militarism that the bureaucratic power mongers are using to oppress the people, but can't seem to find the time to do any pro bono public interest work, as he is too busy being a radical—a full time job.
Adult: Becomes a successful real estate developer/slumlord.
Identifying Call: "Like, the court made another fascist ruling in this case, which does not surprise me at all, man..."

THE PRE-INDICTMENT LINEUP ◻ 101

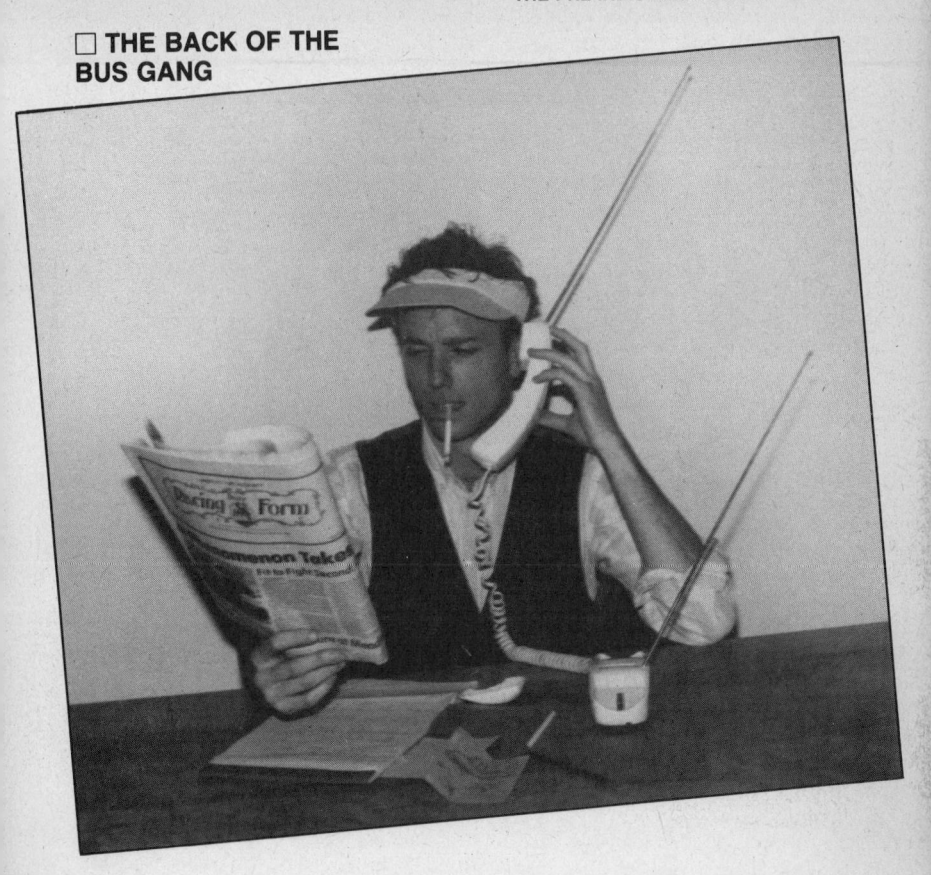

◻ THE BACK OF THE BUS GANG

ROW 4
Thoroughbredus handicapicthes
Markings: Portable hotline to his bookie, handicapping sheet, point spreads.
Characteristics: Exhausted from staying up all night preparing the point spread for this week's football pool. Would have skipped class, but felt a duty to his football pool subscribers. Also an expert handicapper in America's number 2 and 3 favorite sports, thoroughbred racing and Asshole Bingo. Too busy to study, and so undistinguished academically, but aces tax class.
Adult: Gets LL.M. in tax while spending 10 hours a day at the tracks. Becomes famous tax attorney before he is indicted on 2,173 counts.
Identifying call: "Zzzz...What? I told you—Green Bay over...Oh, sorry, Professor Verrall, could you repeat the question? On second thought, the odds are 25 to vs. 3 against that I'll know the answer...I pass."

ROW 4
Tyrannostudentia iconoclasticus
Markings: "Party-mate" beer cooler, stuffed for post-class golf game. Canned briefs, *Playboy* and *High Times* magazines.
Characteristics: Always looks like he's hard at work. He is. He's hard at work writing pornographic briefs, caricatures of the profs, and Asshole Bingo sheets, and figuring his pay-off in the Belmont 500. Attending law school at the insistence of his father, a judge, who otherwise was going to have him arrested. Moderates "College Bowl" series, brings props for everyone (fake mikes, name plates, buzzers, etc.).
Adult: Becomes outrageously successful personal injury litigator profiled in "United States Lawyer" for his ability to "entertain, mesmerize, and captivate" juries and bring in huge verdicts "in a game-show atmosphere." Retires from law to host game show on cable TV.
Identifying call: "Listen, Professor Downs, I'll make you a deal. I'll brief this case if you can tell me who hit the sacrifice fly in last night's double-header against Baltimore."

THE PRE-INDICTMENT LINEUP □ 103

ROW 4
Noblessaurus Obligeiam
Markings: An ounce of high-grade Sensimillan weed, 6 grams of "Aztex Trampoline Dust," Lotus Owner's Manual, "Yachting" and "After Dark" periodicals.
Characteristics: Inherits for a living, so he can't see what all the squabbling is about in collective bargaining lawsuits. Nor can he see why all the Big Firm hopefuls are so obsessed and work so hard. ("I mean, its so...common!") Drama major. Attending Law School because he was fired as a waiter and was threatened with disinheritance. Provides Mercedes (his other car) for road trips. Consistently performs well in "College Bowl."
Adult: Starts a magazine along the line of "Interview" featuring drunken tape-recorded interviews of his (and daddy's) friends. Hailed as "an exciting glimpse of the cutting edge of the New Age." The magazine makes a fortune, exasperating him no end, as he is driven into a higher tax bracket.
Identifying Call: "Moi? Surely you jest! (Don't bogart that joint, you prole)."

ROW 4
Gonzo maniacus psychedelicus
Markings: *National Lampoon*, Party-Mate beer cooler, Walkman, *Atlantic Monthly*, and *Soldier of Fortune*, pint bottle of José Cuervo Gold, lime, salt, knife, mescaline.
Characteristics: Attending law school because he was laid off after welding for two years on the Alaskan pipeline, and his parole officer insisted. Exerts incredible mental effort in class, trying to maintain serenity while surrounded by glowing red pterodactyls the size of Buicks and gargantuan llamas with human heads and seven legs. Has already sent note propositioning redhead in front row, now working on invitation to his Bi-weekly Tropical Soirée/Slam Dance Extravaganza.
Adult: Successful as DA due to ability to get accused felons to admit to their crimes while testifying, although his unorthodox methods of cross-examination (using brass knuckles on witnesses) are frowned upon. Quits to climb Everest, then becomes professional speed-skier. Makes fortune promoting rock 'n' roll "Woodstock" in Aspen. Present whereabouts unknown.
Identifying call: "Could you repeat the question please? I was, um, preoccupied."

☐ THE PROFESSOR: Law School's Most Perfectly Evolved Subspecies

Q: Who is all things to all people: sage, mentor, saint, inquisitor, philosopher, tactitian, stern disciplinarian, indulgent father figure, humorist, moralist, realist, baboon?

    a) Johnny Carson
    b) Your professor

Clearly, both answers are correct, but any discussion of Johnny would involve talking about Ed McMahon, a task that is beyond the scope of this (or any) book. So we will confine our discussion to your professor. He doesn't want to share the limelight anyway.

There is no relationship more complex, passion-ridden, tempestuous, maddening, and gratifying than that between the law student and his professor. Well, perhaps there are a few—Socrates and Plato, Faust and Mephistopheles, Anthony Perkins and his mother in *Psycho*—but those are the perquisite exceptions to the rule.

You will experience a range of emotions at the hands (or the feet) of your professor that you had not thought possible: complete humiliation when he terrorizes you in front of the class, joy and pride when he acknowledges your superior performance, rage and hatred when he gives you a 75 on your test, undying gratitude when he writes you a glowing recommendation, amusement when he wears his purple "shimmer-eaze" tie to class for the 217th time, and frustration when by the end of the year he still has not learned your name.

As with other perverse relationships, the best approach to take here is to follow your emotions, let your conscience be your guide, and remember that while it is an appealing option, manslaughter is a felony punishable by up to 15 years, so think twice.

No chapter on professors would be complete without talking about the professor, at least in passing. This is a shame, because the chapter got off to a good start, and it would be terrific if we could just slide into the next chapter and then head off to happy hour, but such are the demands of comprehensive bookwriting.

So we launch forthwith into "Law School Professor and Phylum Condrycthes: A Comparative Field Guide," published by the Harvard Bio-Evolutionary Department, which traces the evolutionary development (is there any other kind?) of primitive sharks and other cartilaginous battle cruisers into the modern-day law school professor. It is a fascinating guide, and so comprehensive in its detail that we are plagiarizing it word for word right here.

106 □ YOUR WORLD AND WELCOME TO IT

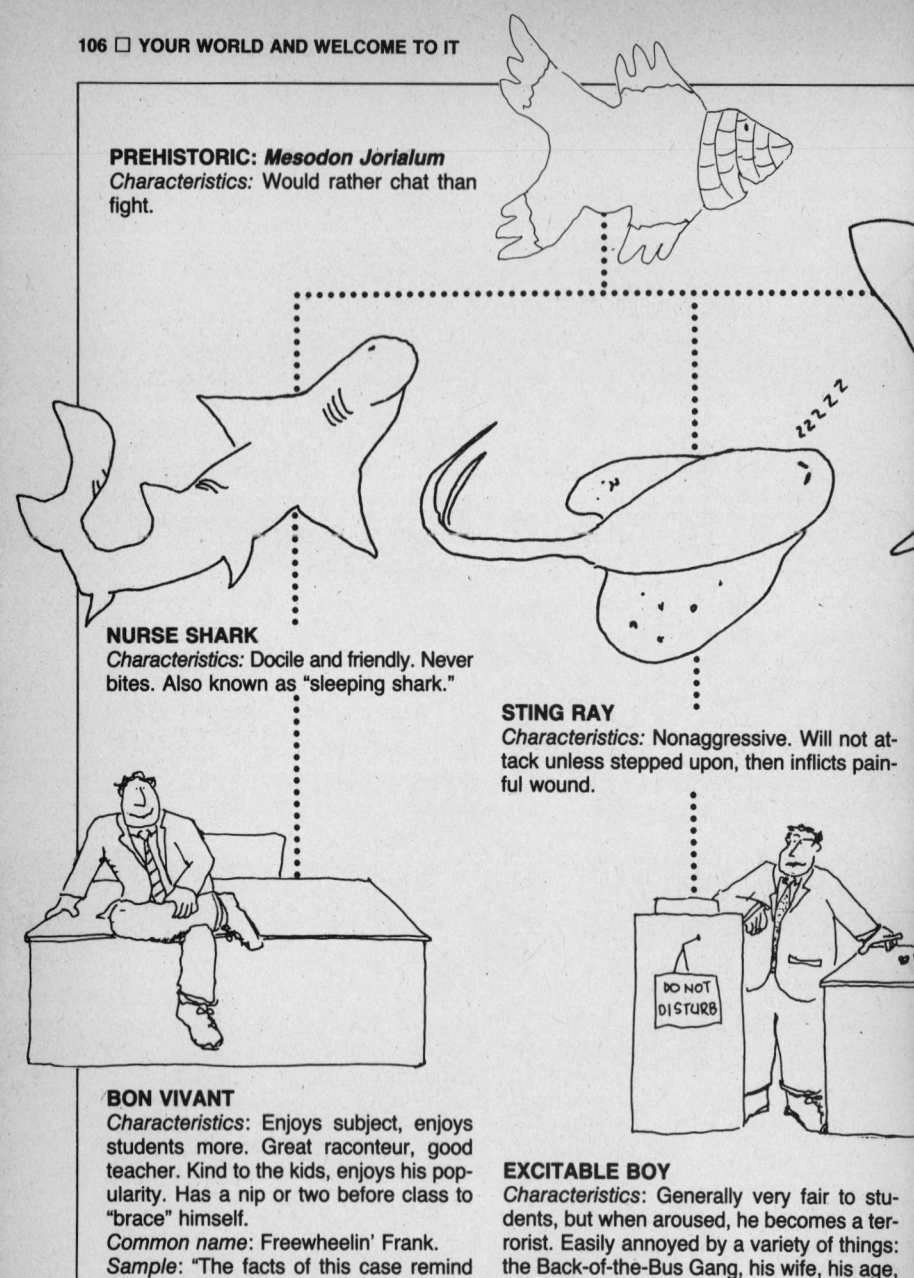

PREHISTORIC: *Mesodon Jorialum*
Characteristics: Would rather chat than fight.

NURSE SHARK
Characteristics: Docile and friendly. Never bites. Also known as "sleeping shark."

STING RAY
Characteristics: Nonaggressive. Will not attack unless stepped upon, then inflicts painful wound.

BON VIVANT
Characteristics: Enjoys subject, enjoys students more. Great raconteur, good teacher. Kind to the kids, enjoys his popularity. Has a nip or two before class to "brace" himself.
Common name: Freewheelin' Frank.
Sample: "The facts of this case remind me of the time we were sailing in the Caribbean..."

EXCITABLE BOY
Characteristics: Generally very fair to students, but when aroused, he becomes a terrorist. Easily annoyed by a variety of things: the Back-of-the-Bus Gang, his wife, his age, the traffic, the weather, etc. When treated with kid gloves, he calms right down.

THE PRE-INDICTMENT LINEUP ☐ 107

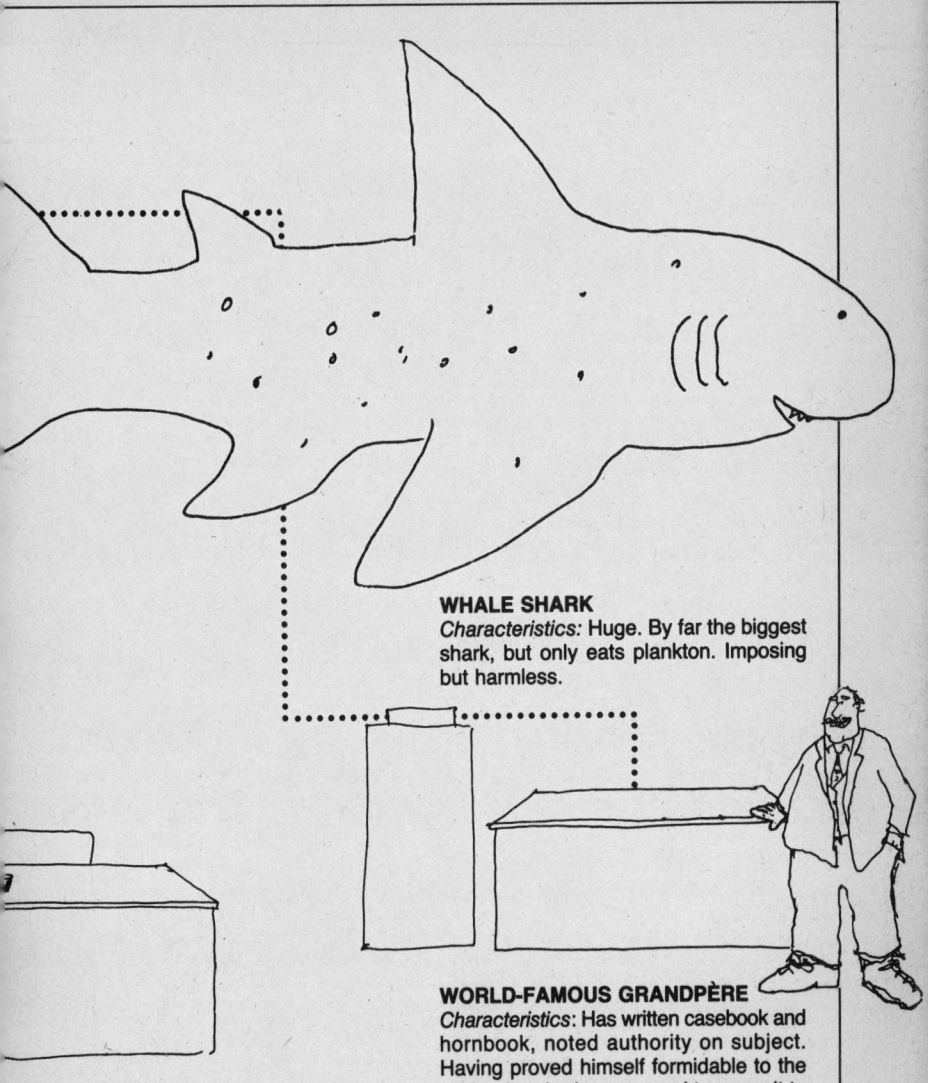

WHALE SHARK
Characteristics: Huge. By far the biggest shark, but only eats plankton. Imposing but harmless.

Common name: Dr. Jekyll.
Sample: "Mr. Jones, you've been whispering up there for the last 5 minutes. Now you're going to get a chance to share it with the class. For the next 45 minutes."

WORLD-FAMOUS GRANDPÈRE
Characteristics: Has written casebook and hornbook, noted authority on subject. Having proved himself formidable to the profession, he has no need to prove it to his students. Solicitous and kind. Everyone continues to write postcards to him when they graduate.
Common name: Grandpa, Uncle Miltie.
Sample: "Very good brief. Now if I could add just one or two points..."

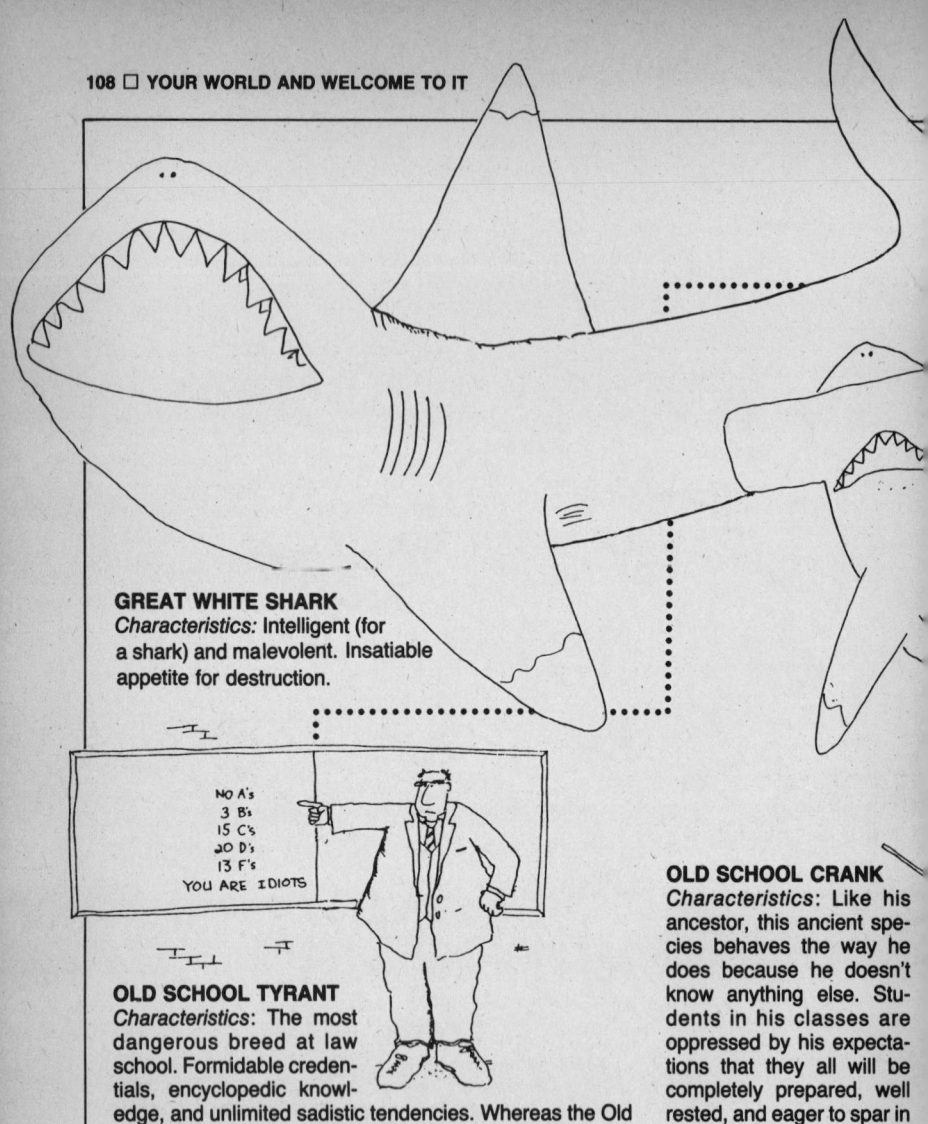

GREAT WHITE SHARK
Characteristics: Intelligent (for a shark) and malevolent. Insatiable appetite for destruction.

OLD SCHOOL TYRANT
Characteristics: The most dangerous breed at law school. Formidable credentials, encyclopedic knowledge, and unlimited sadistic tendencies. Whereas the Old School Crank punishes students out of exasperation and irascability, this prof does it for the sheer thrill of making people suffer. And after 45 years of practice, he is a master at it. Not teaching—just making students miserable. Steer clear of these waters!
Common name: The Executioner, Der Fuehrer.
Sample: "That was a pathetic brief. Suppose you look at your book there and try to tell us what the real issue in this case is. The class can wait. After all, you've already wasted 10 minutes of our time."

OLD SCHOOL CRANK
Characteristics: Like his ancestor, this ancient species behaves the way he does because he doesn't know anything else. Students in his classes are oppressed by his expectations that they all will be completely prepared, well rested, and eager to spar in Socratic pugilistics. He is demanding and stubborn, teaches from memory (he usually wrote the casebook), and is infuriated by the low caliber of students being turned out in the 20th century.
Common name: The Fossil, Professor Blackacre.

THE PRE-INDICTMENT LINEUP □ 109

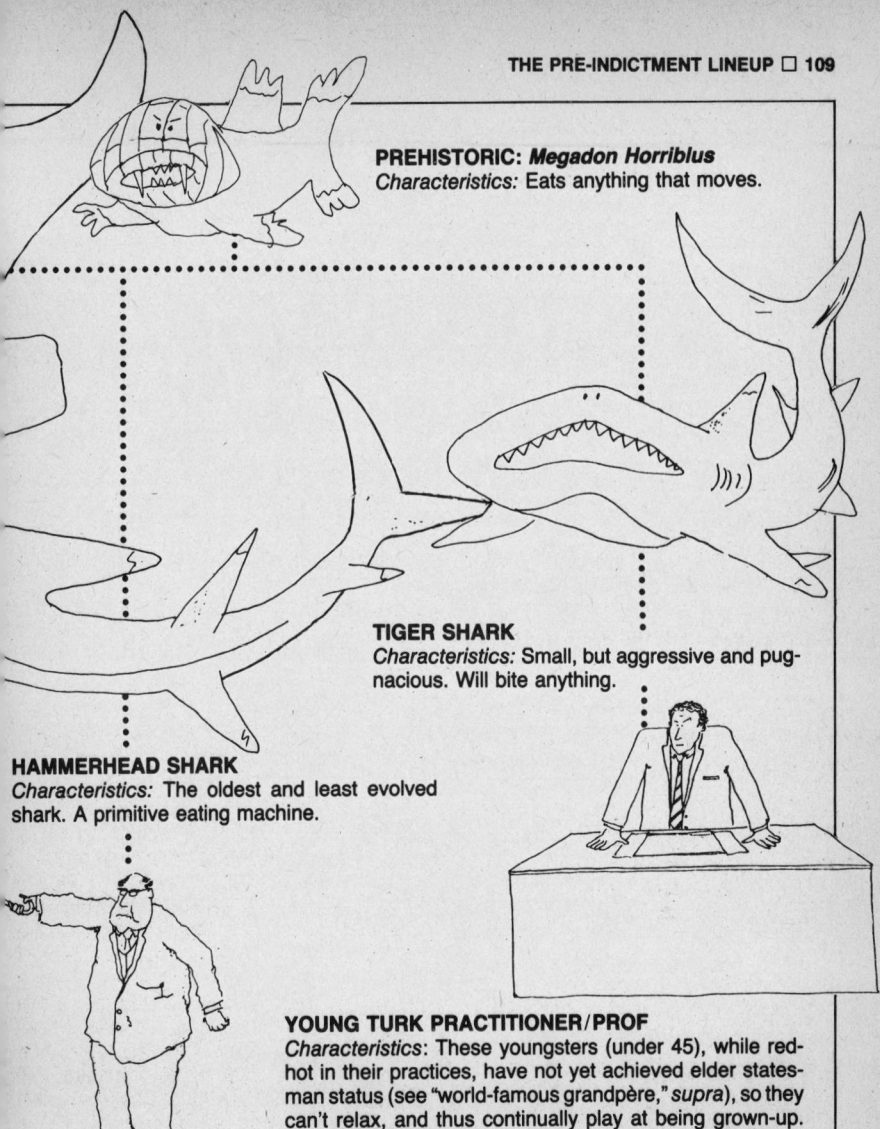

PREHISTORIC: *Megadon Horriblus*
Characteristics: Eats anything that moves.

TIGER SHARK
Characteristics: Small, but aggressive and pugnacious. Will bite anything.

HAMMERHEAD SHARK
Characteristics: The oldest and least evolved shark. A primitive eating machine.

Sample: "Pass? Why, in my day when a student passed, it was tantamount to an admission of idiocy. Why don't you become a blacksmith, boy?"

YOUNG TURK PRACTITIONER/PROF
Characteristics: These youngsters (under 45), while red-hot in their practices, have not yet achieved elder statesman status (see "world-famous grandpère," *supra*), so they can't relax, and thus continually play at being grown-up. Do not breathe a sigh of relief that you have a "younger" prof. They are just as likely to be incredibly aggressive and nasty in class, modeling themselves after the Old School Tyrant, or sympatico with the students, following the Bon Vivant example.
Common name: Wonder Woman, Boy Wonder.
Sample: "Now I assume that you intend to graduate, Ms. Ettinger, so let me give you some advice. *Never* pass in my class."

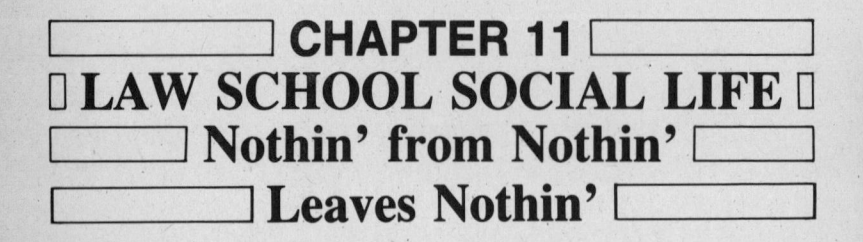

CHAPTER 11
LAW SCHOOL SOCIAL LIFE
Nothin' from Nothin' Leaves Nothin'

Albert Camus, famous existentialist and part-time bon vivant, was once heard to remark, "There are two concepts which strike me as bleak, stark, and utterly without redemption. One is the parking lot behind Trader Vic's when it is empty, and other is the so-called "social life" at most law schools. I cannot contemplate either of these two nihilistic visions without experiencing existential nausea, or at the very least, indigestion." Having said this, he then stuffed his face with deviled eggs and jotted down his thoughts on a napkin (or what he thought was a napkin—it turned out to be the host's three-year old daughter) before bounding off to his study to continue work on his humorous bestseller *The Plague*.

Without wishing to quarrel with our favorite high school philosopher, we must take exception to his slanderous remark. The parking lot at Trader Vic's is sad-looking when it is empty, but hardly nihilistic. And as for law school social life, so what? He doesn't have to go around trumpeting the fact to any stranger he meets at a cocktail party. Some people have no discretion. And all of them are French. What do you think of them apples, Al?

☐ WHERE THE ACTION (Such as It Is) IS

Other than going to the library, which is a veritable Sodom and Gomorrah of unbridled lust and hi-jinx, there are a few activities that allow the young and the restless to spread their wings. Here are the places they spread them.

The Tube

Despite the protestations of professors, a student lounge nowadays will sport, in addition to the traditional paint-by-number "Last Supper" paintings and Day-Glo string art sculptures of Mona Lisa and Daffy Duck, a big, fat color TV. These days TVs are practically immovable fixtures in law school lounges (primarily because they are welded onto the walls to prevent the students from walking off with them).

The programming invariably adheres to the three S's: soaps, *Star Trek*, and Stooges. Students rarely disagree over these choices. It is only when the *General Hospital* groupies are challenged by the *As the World Turns* soapheads that problems occur, and these are usually settled quickly by animated negotiation and a ballpeen hammer.

Soaps are ideal for diversion, as the pace is glacially slow and so allows students time to read cases in between crises. Conversely, or inversely, the characters in the soaps provide the melodrama, psychobabble, and convoluted sexual shenanigans so sorely absent from the average (or above-average) law student's life. And they are instructive in a legal sense—every 10 minutes somebody commits at least three actionable offenses:

TONY: I love you, Sarah. Let's go to bed. [misrepresentation, solicitation, attempted corruption of the morals of a minor]
SARAH: What about your wife, Gretchen?
TONY: Who? Oh, you mean my fiancée. We've broken up. [fraud, nondisclosure, active concealment]
SARAH: Oh, Tony, I don't know what to think. That's not what she told me this morning at your wedding. Oh, what shall I do? [prospective frustration of purpose, seeking further assurances, unconscionable overacting]
TONY: Who cares what she thinks? You drive me wild. And you're here in my house. Let's go upstairs now, or... [duress, false imprisonment, attempted adultery]
SARAH: Tony, let's run off. Where no one will find us. We'll get married. [conspiracy, attempted bigamy, felony-level stupidity]

Trekkies, of course, have been lost in Romulan space since college, and aren't about to give up watching *Star Trek* re-runs just because the academic pace has picked up a little since the good old days of Physics for Poets. Besides, *Star Trek* gives us an idea of how law can work in an ideal universe where men are dressed in pajamas and females from other planets all look like Debbie Reynolds. Basically, any interplanetary holocaust can be averted by getting the queen of the planet and Captain Kirk together at a drive-in for a little nookie. A very just and efficient system.

On the other hand, as prospective lawyers, students must be practical about seeing the law as it is, not as it should be. Hence the popularity of the Three Stooges.

Video Games

It is only fair to tell you that our most noble institutions (and law schools) have officially sanctioned the placement of video games in their lounges. Naturally, such lowbrow entertainment is shunned by serious students, who will rarely spend more than eight hours a day playing them.

Actually, the games have a beneficial invigorating and cathartic effect on the students who play them. This is because *all* of the games feature somebody being chased until he is annihilated. The chasee can fend off his attackers with varying degrees of success, but eventually they speed up, or his time runs out, and "poof." (Well, not necessarily "poof," but some sort of equivalent video death knell.) The emotional merry-go-round a student feels when playing these games (panic, terror, revenge) is precisely identical to how he feels in class throughout law school, so the chance to turn on the demons that pursue him, even for a short time, is a welcome release, even though it is only make-believe.

In-House Dates

Once every few months, an amorous law student will feel his oats and ask a pretty young thing (usually of the opposite gender) out on a date. She will invariably say, "Not until hell freezes over," which, while subject to interpretation, usually means "No." So our student is stuck all alone with his oats. Not a pretty sight. To avoid such outright rejection, and the ensuing heartburn, most canny students will avoid asking for social dates and instead opt for the more acceptable "in-house dates." These dates have the added advantage of involving no outlay of cash; and there is *nothing* a law student likes more than getting a free date.

A typical date involves eating lunch together in the cafeteria and making jokes about the mystery meat. If the potential paramours can still stand each other, they may even play some pinball or video games together. If they have been going steady (to the cafeteria) for a while, one of them may splurge and throw in a quarter to pay for the other person's game. What the hell. You only go through life once, right? Library "study dates" are even more exhilarating, because the mutual sharing of exciting cites can create a real feeling of intimacy. There in the stacks, there are a zillion ways for young romance to burst through the bounds of common decency.

The problem is that it rarely does. And any attempts at real dates (i.e., outside the law school) always result in disaster, for somehow the passion seems to fade as soon as the lovebirds set foot outside of the dark, cool nest where they were, by comparison to the rest of the drones, Zelda and F. Scott Fitzgerald.

Once they hit the harsh light of day and are surrounded by normal, happy people, the relationship crumbles. Each turtledove realizes how incredibly dull her or his partner is, and becomes instantly aware of a hundred different creative ways to spend time (like watching buildings decay, or traffic lights change), none of which involve the other person. For this reason, many loyal couples deliberately flunk so they can remain in never-never land where they will always be the hottest thing going.

☐ HOW TO LIBRARY: A Frisky Guide from the Mezzanine to the Back Stacks and Back

All of the action at law school, be it good, bad, or ugly, takes place at the library. To miss the drama unfolding daily between the front racks and the back stacks is to miss out on the excitement and promise of law school life, social or otherwise.

Because all of the students in the library are secure in the knowledge that they are "studying," they feel a tremendous relief from the guilt and panic that plagues them when they are *not* in the library "studying."

As a result, they feel free to spend hours wandering around, gossiping, attempting to make eye contact with would-be paramours, and, of course, looking for ways to reduce their study load (e.g., steal someone else's outline).

In an effort to ease your culture shock in adapting to this essential environment, we provide a bird's-eye view of the natives at work, at play, and at ease. (See following pages.)

1. Sometimes scoping the scene from the mezzanine can be exhausting—there's so much action to keep track of. In such cases of fatigue, remember: "Anytime can be naptime." When in doubt—get horizontal.

2. Overt propositions are best delivered by air. Air mail lends them a certain panache and allows the propositioner to avoid bodily injury by remaining a discreet distance away from the propositionee, should the latter decide to pummel him.

3. The classic scoping stance—seated at carrel, arms spread, hands gripping railing for stability, leaning forward for maximum peripheral vision.

4. A common hobby has emerged among law students: creative suicide attempts. Here a distraught 1-L tied his shoelaces to the banister and swan-dived over the side. He received an average score, 9.5, from the judging panel (primarily because of the difficulty factor)—a perfect score would have been possible if it had not been for the 8.7 from the East German judge.

5. From time to time, somebody on the mezzanine will "accidentally" knock his coffee or hornbook off the railing, and after it reaches the terminal velocity of 200 feet per second, it will land directly on your head.
A bicycle helmet is always in good taste, and its practical advantages make it all but indispensable. If it saves you from just one hot-coffee avalanche, or a *Federal Reporter* piledriver, it will have earned its keep.

6. *A torrid love story.* They started off studying on opposite sides of the room. After four months of strategic eye contact, he asked if she had *Federal Reporter* 355 for a law review note he was researching. They were young, it was spring, one thing led to another and within six more months, they were sitting at the same table.

7. *The library shower.* No young Romeo would think of wooing his Juliet-to-be without freshening up and putting on his Sunday best. Here, a young Lancelot takes a quick "Lysol bath" in

114 □ YOUR WORLD AND WELCOME TO IT

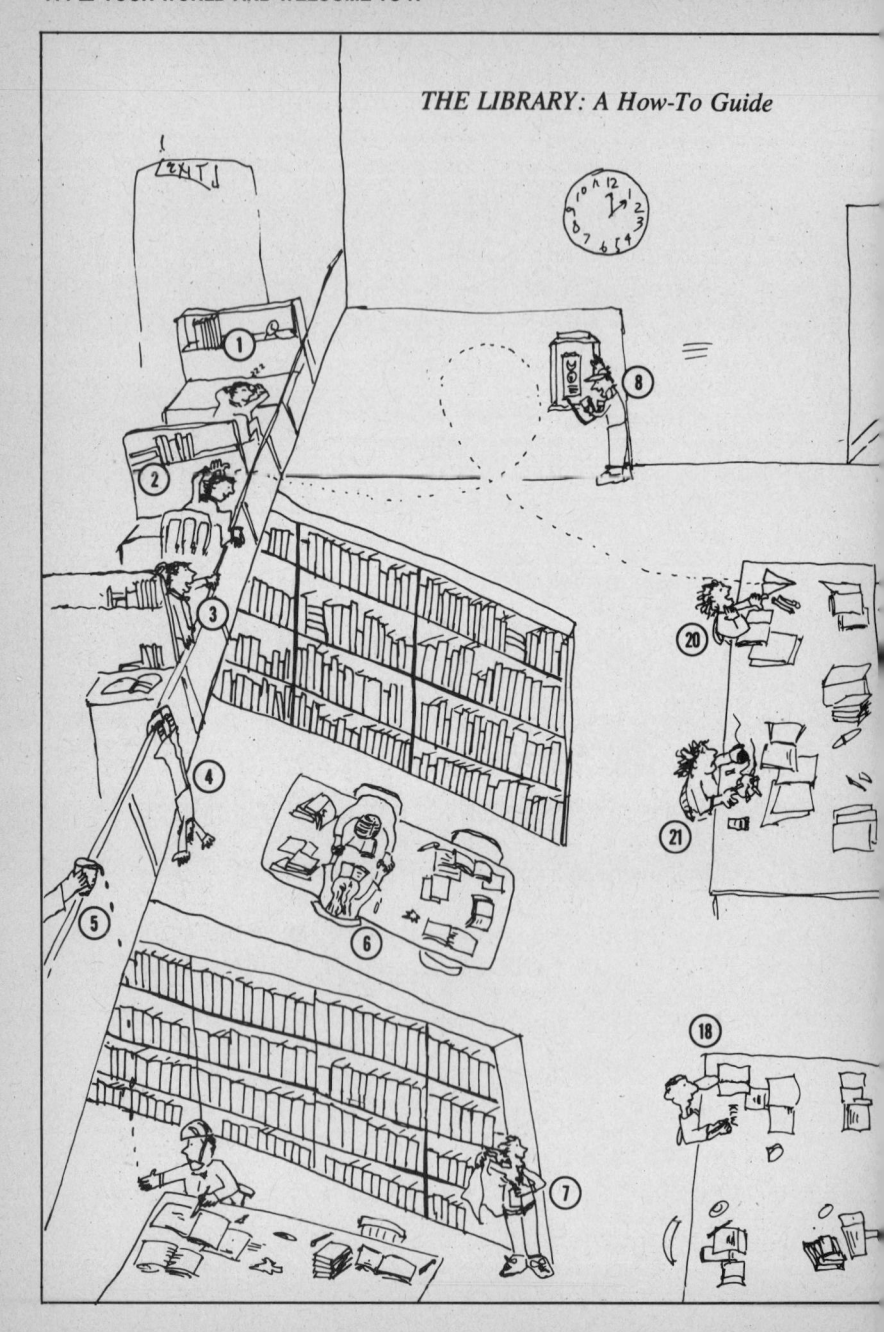

THE LIBRARY: *A How-To Guide*

LAW SCHOOL SOCIAL LIFE ☐ 115

preparation for his first encounter with his Guinevere. As he knows, first impressions are everything!

8. *A day at the races.* When most students talk about "heavy booking," they are usually referring to studying law. To Jake "Numbers" Blino, this is an unjustifiable colloquial intrusion into a well-established and honorable institution. Here, he takes advantage of a study tool that makes his own brand of booking easier: Off-Track Betting. Using OTB, he can take advantage of hot tips without leaving the comfort of his library.

9. *The watering hole.* It's 1:00 a.m. and you need a break from studying. Everything in the building is closed down—except for, you guessed it, the vending machine! It's party time. Studiers can relax and trade gossip, while munching on polyethylene-based cheese puffs.

10. *Happy hour.* Taking a break to unwind, chatty students will spend up to three minutes just "hanging out," trading witticisms about commercial paper.

11. *The happy homesteader.* This red-hot is a homebody deep down. He hopes to acquire his little piece of turf through adverse possession and a Boy Scout tent. He needn't worry about unwanted visitors—the olfactory "wall of silence" will adequately repel any prospective interlopers.

12. *The nineteenth-hour nod.* After 19 hours of power-grinding, some students feel an inexplicable drowsiness. When you feel this coming on despite your caffeine/amphetamine ingestion, don't fight it. Just make sure that before you nod off, you cover your valuables (i.e., notes) and use them for pillows. Remember, the enemy is everywhere.

13. *Self-Help Doctrine #1: The Ol' Fishin' Hole.* This illustrates the folly of nodding off without proper defensive precautions. Because for every Moby Dick study group outline, there is a plucky Ahab just waiting to make it his own. Here, a basic roostertail lure is being used, with 12-pound-test line and a 3-pound weight.

14. *Self-Help Doctrine #2: The "On a Clear Day You Can See Forever" Technique.* This rather unobtrusive and genteel approach allows the patron in the "box seat" to copy from everybody in the orchestra pit, without disrupting anyone. This method is more dependable than the rod 'n' reel approach, especially when the information you desire lies across the room, which would demand highly accurate casts.

15. *Surf 'n' Turf.* Just because you've been torn from the beaches of Santa Monica doesn't mean you have to lose your tan. A chaise-lounge-and-sunlamp combo can help you avoid the library-paste complexion that afflicts all of your fellow cave dwellers.

16. *The Back-of-the-Bus Gang study group.* As everyone knows, an

out-of-the-way corner in the library is a good place to meet with your study group. Having removed a row of *Southwest Reporters* (1954–57) to make way for the bar, these students are now seriously engaged in the exchange of the sort of information so vital to study groups: Rich has just demurrered to Suzy's bet and raised; he thinks she's bluffing. Suzy raises and responds that she never bluffs. Cooch offers the interloctory opinion that she bluffed on the last hand. Willie "the Shoe" points out in his closing argument that he has the aces, so she definitely is bluffing. Now that the legal issues are clear, Suzy folds.

17. *The weight of knowledge*. It's fine to build little fortresses out of the books you are researching; they can provide a necessary sense of security. But beware of structural instability—when this student's tower of babble collapsed, he was buried for three days; no one came to his rescue, of course. He was accidentally freed when another red-hot dug him out while seeking a *Federal Reporter* at the bottom of the pile.

18. *Carving out a name for yourself*. Old habits die hard, especially for New Yorkers. Here a graffiti artist carves initials into the table. They are not his initials—they are the initials of his rival nominee for Law Review Editor, whom he will dutifully report and prosecute for defacing law school property.

19. The only time Frankie sets foot in the library is when he passes through to hand out invitations for his latest biweekly Fellini *Satyricon* Theme Bash—the only record worse than his library attendance is his classroom attendance. But his fellow students love him for giving them an excuse to stop studying.

20. *The Mailbox Rule*. Melissa ponders the ramifications of Ken's offer for a date—was it effective on dispatch or receipt? Likewise, will her reply ("You're dreaming, rotisserie breath") be effective when she crumples up the paper, or when she throws her books at him?

21. *High anxiety*. Anxious over the massive amount of work confronting him, Danny prepared for 28 straight hours by ramming down a nicotine, amphetamine, Benzedrine cocktail. Unfortunately, he miscalculated the doses, and now is catatonic except for his hands, which are sweating, and his eyes, which are rolling.

CHAPTER 12
LAW REVIEW
How to Become the Crème de la Crème

It is sad, but true: There is Law Review, and there is everything else. Of course, "everything else" encompasses a wide range of goodies which will be denied to the run-of-the-mill Articles Editor, including 5-to-1 tax shelters, brazen hussies draped in the furs of your choice, Cadillac agencies in New Canaan, and human friends. Nevertheless, it is important to bear in mind that Law Review is the Golden Ring of law school; that members of that elite circle will make tons of money right off the bat; and that outside of the Club, there are only huddled masses yearning to be rich. Then again, there are drawbacks to the Law Review life. Members of the Law Review tend to lack social skills common to most primates, they suffer from acute afflictions of buffalo breath, and they score less frequently than the Mets in key situations. But for those of you who feel that a blonde on your arm is small comfort for missing out on the prestige of Law Review, read on.

☐ MAKING LAW REVIEW: The Necessary Legal Pedigree

Making Law Review is as easy as making Mother Theresa in a singles bar on Good Friday afternoon. You simply put your head down and crank for nine months, produce a brilliant series of final exams, and show up in the top 10% of your law school class after the first year. Piece of cake.

Some schools make accommodations for those whose raw intellectual ability is less than overpowering; they permit a select few to join on the basis of a writing competition. Experience suggests that the most successful style includes stapling a $100 bill to the essay. Smaller denominations are recommended if there is to be more than one reader. Such writing competitions are easygoing, free-spirited affairs where aspiring students help one another with research, exchange ideas and insights on common top-

LAW SCHOOL SOCIAL LIFE □ 119

□ LAW REVIEW EDITORS

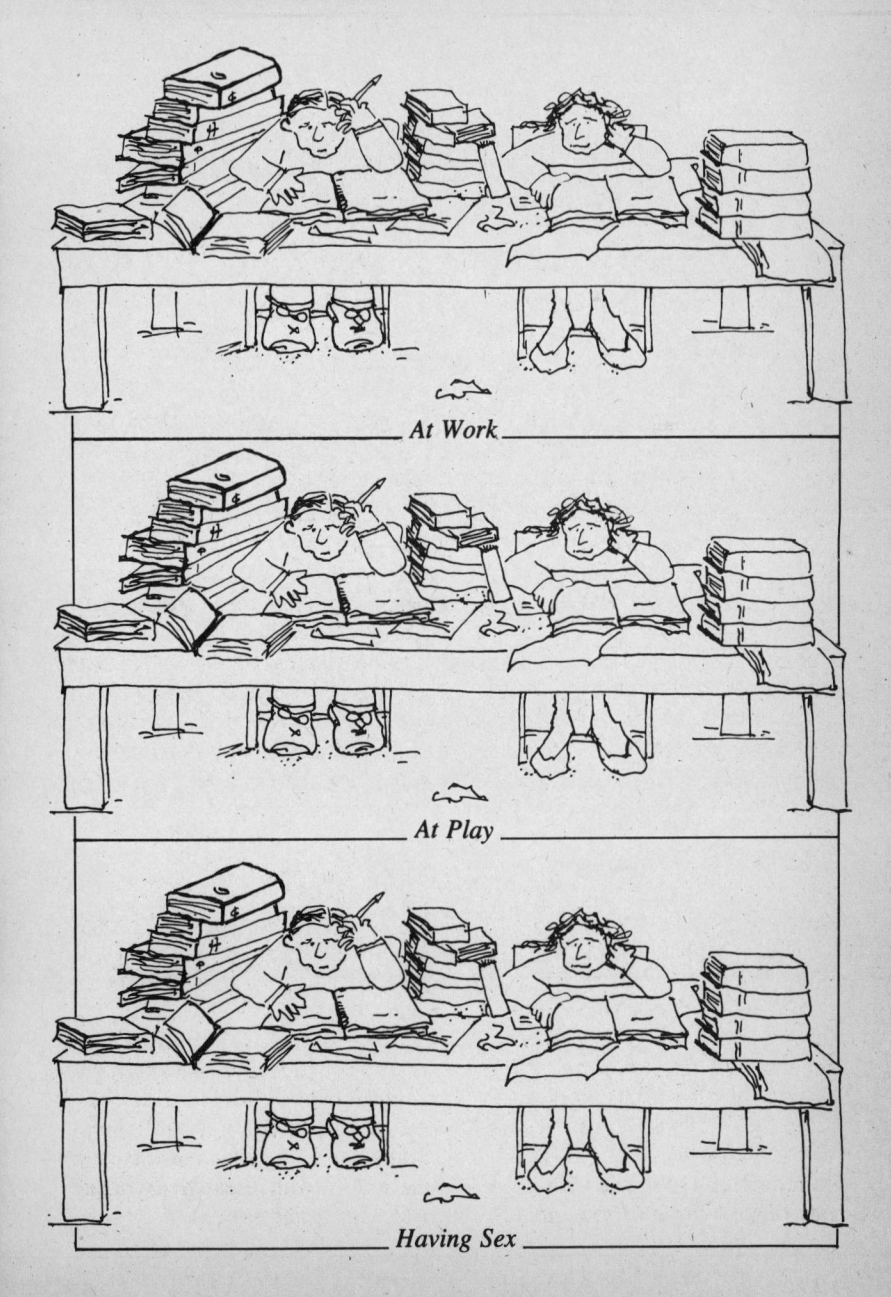

At Work

At Play

Having Sex

ics, and emphasize camaraderie as opposed to competition.*

But whether you take the high road or law road to Law Review, certain things are *de rigueur* if you intend to be successful: proper dress, proper behavior, and proper personal hygiene. Adherence to these strict pre-Law Review requirements is not easy, particularly since the EPA has ruled all three environmentally unsound, and at one school even went so far as to have seven Law Review editors condemned as health hazards (they were then sold at a sheriff's auction to a Mrs. MacIsaacs and are now being employed by her exterminating company as outdoor insect-repellent sticks).

Dressed to Kill: The Law Review Aspirant

For most law students, law school dress is a simple extension of the college ensemble: comfortable jeans, a casual knit shirt, a trendy sweater in solid colors, and comfortable shoes. Aspiring to Law Review, however, requires a bit more. The hair shirt is a medieval standby; ashes and sackcloth may also fill the bill, albeit a tad melodramatically. But in this day and age, access to these time-tested favorites may be limited. Accordingly, we have compiled a small checklist (just like summer camp!) to assist you. For the men—black oxfords (unshined), a lime-green shirt with gullwing collar, blue plaid pants, tan socks, and a maroon windbreaker. For the ladies—same as above; more discretion as to color of windbreaker. If the shirt does not come with a Plasti-pocket pen guard (Nerd-pac), you will be obliged to buy one if you are to remain in step with Law Review haute couture.

In addition to the bold fashion statement they represent, plastic pocket protectors are eminently practical as well. They will keep

LAW REVIEW:
Tomorrow Belongs to Us.
Nattily attired Law Review Editor Norton "Nibs" Poltroon on his way to the library.

---

*Much like the camaraderie of barracuda frenzies, dogfights, gang wars, and New York City traffic jams.

your orange highlighters from staining your shirt (quelle clash!) and protect it from your X-acto knife (indispensable for cutting critical cases out of library books—a time-honored competitive tradition at good schools).

Barring polyethelene-shirt fires started by lit cigarettes, your shirt/slack ensemble should have a polymer half-life of 3,000 years. Why shorten it by washing? All kidding aside—don't wash. Taking the oath of nonablution will enhance your chances of making Law Review, because the editors will be impressed by your commitment, and you will intimidate the competition (and everyone else with olfactory senses) for the same reason.

Cocktail Chatter for the Review Aspirant
Those of you who will succeed will not be likely to be invited to parties of any kind. Your own parties will be sparsely attended; none will be memorable; you will be lucky to get up a game of solitaire. But on the off chance you might stumble into a civilized social situation, we have prepared a small guide to assist.

Do: use the napkin, not your sleeve; mention to every good-looking girl that you've seen her in your Contracts class and that you're surprised a woman who looks so much like Charo could have so much interest in *Hadley* v. *Baxendale*; downplay your interest in law school, and confide that you see yourself as being in transition from Malibu lifeguard to humanist philosopher.

Do Not: say anything else; you're already pushing your luck.

Staying on Law Review
Once you have been initiated into the Golden Circle, you will not lose your savoir faire. You never had any to begin with. Aside from the nasty business of cite-checking (a dirty job; make them up if you have to), and groveling before a third-year law

KNOW YOUR LAW REVIEW: Part 2
A frisky male editor, flushed with the exuberance of youth, gambols with unrestrained glee, unaware of our telephoto lens.

student with galloping acne and an irrational fear of split infinitives, you have nothing to fear but your own lack of grace. And that, as they say in Chem class, is a known quantity.

☐ MOOT COURT: The Unkindest Cut of All

After Law Review has skimmed off the cream of the class, moot court ferments the remainder into sour-tasting cheese. Moot court is mandatory if you don't make the Review. In some schools it is mandatory even if you do. There is nothing at all elite about moot court.

The typical moot court experience.

Since doing well on your moot court appeal can't help you (it is not counted toward your average even if graded, and it is rarely graded), and doing poorly can ruin you (i.e., you have to take it over again), it is small wonder that students have a distaste that borders on phlebitis when recalling the experience. The moot court experience can be summarized thus:

1. *Get topic.* The issue will be based on a curent case up for appeal. You will be assigned as counsel for either appellant or respondent.
2. *Do research.* Tons of it.
3. *Write Brief.* You will have a student "adviser" who will attempt to bust your chops while pretending to "help" you with this part. Why else would anyone voluntarily sign up for this pointless job?
4. *Argue appeal in moot court.* Here you get to play grown-up. Everybody gets dressed up and checks into a "courtroom" (either an unused room at the local federal courthouse or a rented motel room). The three judges are usually Supreme Court judges, local attorneys, waitresses, disk jockeys, or Spandex salesmen.

The object here is to avoid getting carried away. One student was cited for Moot Contempt of Court and was thrown by the Moot Bailiff into Moot Jail in lieu of $60 Moot Bail. So keep it moot clean. A favorite move, although it is not looked upon kindly by moot court, is to leave a foldout from *Hustler* on the podium after your oral argument, just on the outside hope that your opponents will have enough human characteristics to react with shock, or *something*.

National Moot Court competition.

This is a last-chance, 1000-to-1 shot for red-hots who did not make Law Review but are desperate to get into a big firm. To win, you must complete the moot court appeal process (based on the chosen topic) and do better than everyone else in every law school across the country. And they, like you, are trying *very* hard.

In retrospect, it would probably have been easier to get on Law Review. But because it *is* so tough to excel in this competition, National

Moot Court carries the résumé status of making Law Review, and if you can pull your grades up to the top 10% by the end of second year, too, you may be back on the fast track.

GREAT MOMENTS IN MOOT COURT HISTORY
The Wilkins-Cruze Appellant team, having concluded oral argument, leave memento on podium for Armand Deal, Respondent—a Penthouse centerfold (which turns out to be Miss April, Armand's favorite).

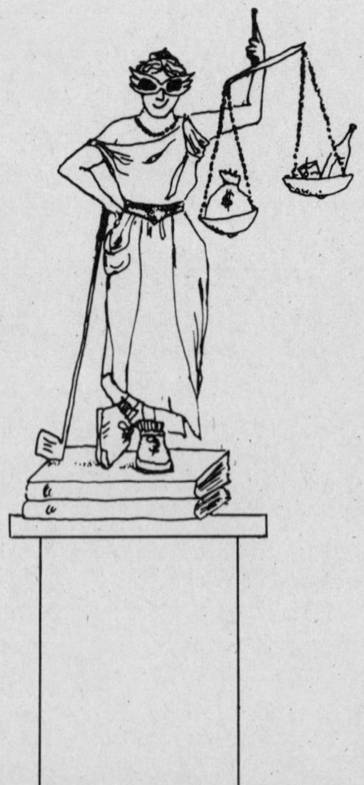

SECTION IV
THE TRIALS OF JOB
From Interview to Offer in Three Easy Kung-Fu Moves

Your interviewer will be affable, friendly, and genuinely interested in you as a person.

CHAPTER 13
OFFENSIVE INTERVIEWING
"I am in the top 10% of my class, I'm on Law Review, I love your firm, and this gun is loaded."

What? Law firm interviews already? It seems like only yesterday that you forged your college transcripts and recommendations to get into law school. My, time certainly does fly, doesn't it, when one is having such a terrific time, developing a nervous tic, terminal myopia, and the body odor of a wildebeest.

So all of those résumés have come home to roost—you have 14 interviews. Terrific! Sure, there will be a few tense moments as you try to explain how you were appointed to the U.S. Supreme Court during your first year of school for a short time and chose to step down, all without the interviewer's knowledge, or how you managed to clerk for a district court judge who has been deceased since your sixth birthday, but you can blame your resumé typist. ("She's such a kidder, that Ethel!")

Now all that remains is to attend the interview and confront your (possible) employer-to-be, armed with nothing more than a natty J. Press suit, a confident smile, a firm handshake, and a semiautomatic 9mm German Luger. Natural ability, personality, and aplomb will take care of the rest, right?

Wrong, Mescali Mouth! Believe it or don't, the interview is won or lost long before you face your opponent across the desk. As Lucretia Borgia used to say, "Preparation is everything." Remember the Republican convention? Think of how fresh and inspiring it was when certain Young Republicans, unable to control their youthful emotions any longer, burst into spontaneous pro-Nixon cheers, igniting the rest of the crowd!

Now, do you think that all those impromptu eruptions of youthful exuberance would have been anywhere near as recklessly impulsive without the detailed, minute-by-minute computerized itinerary provided for the youngsters? Or the chartered planes to shuttle those "spontaneous cheerers" (the youthful Republicans whose uncontrollable individual outbursts miraculously coincided with the accuracy of a Navy clock) back and forth to convention sites? No, no, no, nyet!

So learn from the pros. At the interview, your "off-the-cuff" questions to the interviewer and your "spur of the moment" answers to his "spontaneous" queries should be natural and impremeditated—as unpremeditated as D-Day was. With this in mind, let's examine the olympic event which you will have a year to prepare for and 20 minutes to perform. Just follow our training program and you'll be ready for the gold when your turn comes.

☐ THE INTERVIEW

The Summer Associate interview is the single most important project you will undertake at law school. Your performance here will determine whether you are on the fast track to success as a lawyer or should go back to being a Hell's Angel. Think of it as a mini-trial. If you are prepared, confident, and smooth, you win. If you are unprepared and defensive, you will be toyed with mercilessly, then sent to the Wall.

Therefore, before you ever face your interviewer, you must have already done your homework by asking and answering the questions that determine whether a particular firm is right for you, and vice versa. Does the firm accept bribes? This will have

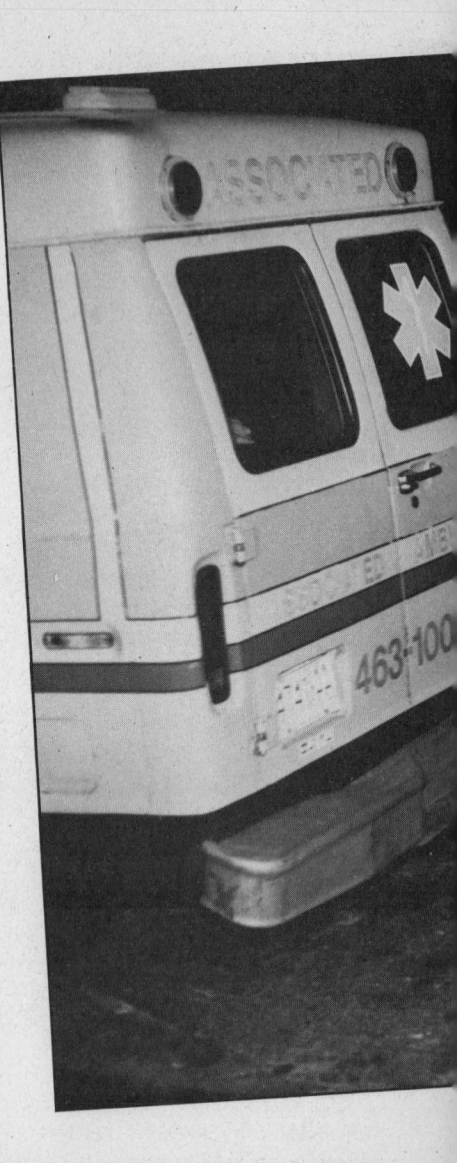

OFFENSIVE INTERVIEWING □ 129

KNOW YOUR FIRM'S SPECIALTY: GREAT MOMENTS IN CLIENT CONTACT HISTORY Mel "Swifty" Blinkoff, Personal Injury Specialist, closes in on his fourteenth contingency fee client of the day at 11:30 P.M. Visibly winded, Mel asserts, "A good lawyer is not a 9 to 5 guy."

a direct bearing on your interview technique. Does the firm specialize in defending the civil rights of old ladies? Or does it specialize in evicting them onto the streets during the winter? This sort of information is critical to your performance—and success—in the subsequent interview.

Knowing a firm inside out is a prerequisite to winning the interview. When the partner asks, "What can I tell you about the firm?" he's not doing that because he wants to answer a lot of questions; he wants to find out whether you've researched adequately prior to the interview. If you haven't bothered to find out about the firm in depth *before* it hires you, how good will you be at researching cases *after* it hires you?

To do well, you must convince the interviewer through your statements, body language, and questions that you are bright, articulate, and hardworking, and that it has always been your life's goal to work for his or her firm. Of *course* he knows that you are interviewing with other firms. But your ability to portray an interviewer's firm as your one and only is as important to interviewers as any of your other skills. Lawyers *love* feigned sincerity— that's what the law *is*, remember?

THE SECRET INTERVIEW

As in any good soap opera, the seemingly mundane dialogue in an interview disguises the titanic struggle that is going on underneath. It's

Your interviewer will be genial and genuinely interested in you as a person.

hard to feign sincerity successfully if you're not even sure just what it is you're being asked. Toward this end, we have translated the typical partner's bland questions, exposing what he is *really* asking you.

Q. "How would you describe yourself? What do you really want to do in life?" ("Are you one of those Ivy League liberal arts victims who went to law school because the Peace Corps wasn't hiring at the time, or have you wanted to be a lawyer ever since the doctor slapped you?")

Q. "What are your long- and short-term career goals and objectives, when and why did you establish these goals, and how are you preparing yourself to achieve them?" ("Can we count on eight years of 18-hour days out of you, or are you going to flake out and join a juggling troupe somewhere like our last associate?")

Q. "What qualifications do you have that make you think you will be successful in the law?" ("I used your résumé to catch the drips from my pastrami sandwich. Can you give me a synopsis of your life so far without boring me to tears?")

Q. "In what ways do you think you can make a contribution to our firm?" ("Do you enjoy doing research until the sun comes up? Are you well connected with megabuck clients?")

"Could you explain the grading system here to me?" ("All these goddam Ivy League schools have switched to pass nonpass. *Are* you in the top 5% of your class or *aren't* you?")

Q. "Do you think your grades are a good indication of your achievement?" ("Are you going to acknowledge that two years of law school performance is a better indicator of talent then a half-hour interview, or am I going to be treated to some whining excuse?")

Q. "What extracurricular activities do you enjoy?" ("Do you have any interest other than word-crunching at a law firm, and if so, are you ready to give it up forever as soon as we hire you?")

Q. "In what kind of environment are you the most comfortable?" ("Am I going to be able to stick you in an office, give you 30 assignments, and forget about you, or are you going to disrupt everyone else by trying to 'relate' with them on a 'human' level?")

Q. "Why did you decide to seek a position with our firm?" ("Look. I know why you're talking to us and 36 other firms—you're starving, and your student loan is coming due. How slick are you at convincing me that you and our firm is a match made in heaven?")

▢ INTERVIEWING THE INTERVIEWER

At some point in the interview (usually at the end), the partner will turn to you and say, "Do you have any questions I can answer for you?"

This is a signal that he is satisfied with your answers thus far, and is now ready for Stage Two of the interview. In Stage Two, both parties engage in a mutual charade where you pretend that you are asking questions to determine whether the firm is fit for you, which is something like an unknown artist interviewing the Nobel Prize Committee to see if he wants to give them his name. The interviewer, in turn, pretends to have genuine concern as to whether the firm fits your goals, when he knows in reality that he could answer your every query with a louder-than-average belch and you would say, "That's *exactly* what I'm looking for."

A silly ritual, perhaps, but one that can make or break an interview. For example, one naive applicant asked a partner if he was happy and felt fulfilled by what he was doing. The partner blanched, gagged, and then burst into tears. Needless to say, no offer there. So avoid such excruciating faux pas—memorize the following tried-and-true questions, and you'll be fine. And if you frame your questions by saying, "My research on your firm led me to believe so, but I'm gratified to hear it is true. Now what about..." (go on to question 2), we can virtually guarantee your success.

1. "What is your method of training your associates? Are they usually assigned to one partner or do you have a rotating system?" (This is good for a large firm.)
2. "If I develop strong preferences in the course of my association with the firm, would there be a reasonable chance that I'd be allowed some exposure to it?" (Nice question—preserves the illusion that you have any choice in the matter, yet is vague enough that he can always answer "Yes" to avoid embarrassing you without committing himself.)
3. "Are you looking for any specific professional interests on the part of associates?" (Be prepared to leap enthusiastically at whatever field he answers.)
4. "Generally, how long does it take an associate to become a partner in your firm?" (This shows him that you're a red-hot and also allows him to brag: "Usually it takes six years, but I got lucky and made it in four," etc.)
5. "How closely will I be supervised in your firm? Will I get a chance to appear in court within a year?" (Obviously, this is only if you are interested in litigation.) "How much responsibility can an associate get if she does well?" (Great—shows how ambitious you are.)
6. "Is your firm still involved in the [*Five Unnamed Plantiffs* v. *Katz Delicatessen*] case? (Shows off the fruits of your in-depth research on his firm—he'll love it.)

☐ BODY LANGUAGE: How to Read Your Interviewers Like a (Tawdry) Book

During the interview, watch your interviewer closely. Does she lean

OFFENSIVE INTERVIEWING ▫ 133

back in her chair? Does he cross his legs? Is he drooling on his tie? These subtle clues, properly recognized and interpreted, provide an unerring psychological gauge which will enable you to size up your interrogator, beat him at his own game, and walk away with a window office and 50 grand a year.

Pay careful attention to the following scenarios depicting typical interview situations. Note the interviewer's body language and the explanations. If you become sufficiently adept enough at recognizing these personal physical idiosyncrasies, the interview will be in your hands—the interviewer will give away all of his secrets without realizing it!

☐ Note the relaxed position of the interviewer; the feet up on the desk to improve circulation, the head tilted back. This interviewer is asleep. If he was in this position when you came in, great. Let him sleep and call him later thanking him for accepting you. He'll be too embarrassed to deny it. If, however, he started the interview awake and alert and gradually assumed this position as you read verbatim from your Law Review note, you're in trouble. In this case, you should think about using your soporific talent to become a law school professor instead.

☐ It is clear from this picture what is going on in the interview. The interviewer has the student in a full hammerlock and is giving him a Power Noogie on the top of his head. The student has just finished boasting about withholding rent for two years with a cleverly constructed "constructive eviction" theory, but it turns out that the partner owns the building. This hammerlock/Noogie combo, coupled with the interviewer's homicidal expression, indicate that the student should forget about getting the offer and should concentrate on getting out of the office alive.

☐ As you can see, the interviewer is on his knees, lighting the student's cigar and asking him whether $53,000 a year would be too low a starting salary. The student is relaxed, as indicated by his position, and is accepting the interviewer's offer of a light with the proper blend of perfunctory gratitude and noblesse oblige.

Their body English indicates that the interviewer, a senior associate at Murphy & Murphy, has been given the assignment of interviewing William Murphy III, or, more specifically, informing young Bill of his starting salary (as determined by head partners William Murphy, Sr., and William Murphy, Jr.) and asking whether Bill III would like his office. Bill will politely accept the salary and gracefully decline the office.

☐ As this picture indicates, the interviewer has stopped taking notes and has put on a Groucho Marx disguise. He is engaging in the "Polish ear-flapperoo" accompanied by a mouth-sound commonly known as a "raspberry." These are subtle warning signs which the observant interviewee should not overlook.

While there are many interpretations possible here, one thing is clear. The student should be on guard that the interviewer is expressing skepticism about the student's qualifications for the firm. While this is not a fatal sign, it indicates that the student has to regain the interviewer's confidence soon, or the interview could end up in the "hammerlock/Noogie" decision, an outcome to be avoided at all costs.

SEIZING THE INITIATIVE

Through proper use of body language, a student applicant can greatly enhance his or her chance of walking away from the interview with an offer in hand. Study the following time-honored techniques. They are subtle, and will not be consciously noticed by the interviewer, but each technique is designed to subliminally influence the interviewer's subconscious feelings about the student, resulting in that all-important offer!

☐ Notice how the student has artfully "broken the ice" here by placing his briefcase on the desk and putting his hand on the interviewer's shoulder. The effectiveness of these moves is enhanced by the stacks of $20 and $50 bills which are bulging out of the open briefcase.

Remember what we said about nuance? Well, here is a prime example. It is not necessary for the student to point out the cash. As if by magic, those neatly ordered rows of Thomas Jeffersons will catch the attention of the interviewer's subconscious. They will conduct an exceedingly friendly interview and the student will forget to take his briefcase when he leaves. He will receive a call from the partner within the week confirming the offer and adding, "By the way, you left your empty briefcase at the interview — my secretary is holding it for you. Let's go out to lunch tomorrow."

tinent questions about the firm. In fact, she will have to ask *all* of the questions as she has rendered the partner incapable of doing anything except nodding yes or no. The proper question here is "Are you going to make me an offer or do I make like a Cuisinart?" This forces the interviewer to nod yes and shake his head no in rapid succession, an attempt most students find highly amusing. What he is trying to convey is "Congratulations — you have the offer; welcome to the team!"

☐ It is well known that the person sitting behind the desk has an advantage in the body language balance of power. Notice how adroitly our applicant has reversed the balance in this scene by circling the desk and placing her right knee in the small of the interviewer's back, while gagging him with a regulation G.I. Issue garrote ($13.95 at Army/Navy surplus stores). This maneuver was prompted by the partner's asking her, "What is your typing speed and how well do you take dictation?"

The interviewee is now in a position to assert herself by asking per-

☐ Here, our applicant is using body language along with props (specifically, a telescoping pointer and a financial chart of her daddy's Fortune 500 company) to convey to the interviewer that she would be an asset to the firm. This subtle maneuver is convincing the interviewer that she is a good researcher and an effective speaker (he will notice how the chart gets her point across without a lot of verbiage: "Legal fees...$4.3 million").

She reinforces her body language verbally by saying, "You know, Daddy's not really happy with the company's present law firm. He's asked my advice, but I want to wait until I'm sure before I tell him what firm to go with." She will be accepted as soon as she completes the sentence.

☐ Notice here how the student's body language is nicely complemented by his six-foot-two companions. They are nattily attired in oversized trenchcoats with large telltale bulges in their coat pockets.

The interviewer has asked the gentlemen if they would like to sit down. They reply no they don't want to sit down, and tell Don, Jr. (our plucky applicant) to get on with it so they can go back to work. Obligingly, he turns to the partner and says, "Now, about that job..." The interviewer accepts immediately. This is possibly due to the partner's subconscious desire to be liked by everyone. [Note: While Italian companions are preferable, any behemoths will do.]

☐ Once in a while, a student will have the luxury of an interview where he doesn't give a damn about the outcome, either because he was already accepted elsewhere or he has just won $4 million at the WINGO lottery.

In this case, the technique is to gather a crowd of peers around the door and then give them a show. The move should be timed for maximum laughs (the more mortified the interviewer is, the bigger the laffs). While in this scenario a Basic Indoor Flash was used, any suitably irreverent body language will suffice. Other favorites are the Double-Bird, the Full Moon, and the Grand Wazoo. Note: While this technique guarantees laughs 100% of the time, it resulted in only 17% offers (slightly higher for women). So use it for laughs only.

☐ **HOW TO HANDLE REJECTION**

What happened? Your résumé is stellar, you were invited to interview with 30 firms, you dressed properly, deftly fielded the questions with ease and savoir faire, and invited each interviewer out to your house in Newport "afterward," an invitation which each accepted eagerly. And now you are sitting on a pile of letters that regret to inform you that this summer you are going to be forced to continue to rely on your trust-fund income, which is already perilously close to dipping under six figures a year. What went wrong?

There is no way to tell why a firm accepts one applicant and rejects another equally qualified applicant. There are simply too many hidden variables. For instance, one red-hot student was shocked to find that she had been turned down by her chosen firm, and it was only years later, through friends who worked there, that she discovered that it was the interviewer who had done it. As it turned out, he misunderstood her when she playfully referred to him during the interview as a "fat, greasy, pizza-faced fascist pig." Now, how was she to know that he was having a bad day that day and would react unreasonably? You can't know everything.

So don't blame yourself. Maybe your competition taped bigger bills to their résumés, or committed acts which we won't even go into here because we're not that kind of book. (For $12.50, however, you can get a complete list, with color photographs, from the author. He is that kind of guy.) The first thing to remember is, "It's their fault." These firms, which you thought were populated by intelligent people, just passed up the bargain of a lifetime, a diamond in the rough, a silk purse, a ray of sunshine, the silver lining, perhaps that last hope for mankind, in short, you—because they were (pick any number of the following adjectives that you feel apply):

fascist	clonelike	mechanistic
myopic	simplistic	cowardly
sexist	sadistic	swinish
cheap	lowbrow	demented
biased	shallow	alcoholic
tawdry	stupid	bucolic
disgusting	nepotistic	misinformed
conformist	racist	

So they blew it. Let's face it. But it would be unfair of you not to give them a second chance, or at the very least, give them the dignity of a response. Let the following tips be your guide in this endeavor of social grace:

The "I didn't hear that" response
After receiving the rejection letter, write to the hiring partner, saying in substance, "I have not yet received a letter from your firm, which I am most eager to join. By the way, I saw your wife picking up your two kids from kindergarten. Cute kids—it sure would be awful if something happened to them. Well, hope to hear from you soon!"

The Rejection Letter Rejection Letter
This should be on your letterhead stationery, and should employ the same solicitous tone as that used in the rejection letter.

Perhaps you wish to avoid the cold formality of a letter, and would prefer to deliver your reaction to the rejection in person. Good idea: It is much more intimate and allows a

> Dear Mr. Hampton:
> Thank you for your rejection letter. It was certainly a thoughtful and impressive one. We're sorry, but due to the large number of equally qualified rejection letters we have received this interviewing season, we are unable to accept your rejection letter. Please feel free to send us a rejection letter next year when we may have a place for it. We will keep a copy of your present one on file. Best of luck to you with your other rejection letters!
> Sincerely,
> Eduardo "Don't Call Me Eddie" Gomez

meaningful exchange between you and your rejector. Some good ones to try are—:

Tae Kwan Do Throat Kick
Obviously any violent martial art form will do here. And other parts of the partner's body are equally acceptable. If you can sense during the interview that the interviewer is going to torpedo you, don't wait for the letter—spontaneity counts!

Banzai Charge
In this perky variation of the bomb threat, you rush into the partner's office with a grenade in your teeth and handcuff yourself to him. You then wail that if he doesn't reconsider, you'll "just die." He will not fail to notice your physical proximity to him, and will suddenly be filled with compassion for your plight.

Rejection Letter Wallpapering
If you have interpreted the small mountain of rejection letters as a sign from God that you should go back to your first love, art, then you are in luck. Your first oeuvre should be a collage/gouache in which you completely cover all of your walls with rejection letters. Then call *People* magazine (which loves to print pictures that graphically depict professional unemployment) and announce your new career.

CHAPTER 14
THE BIG FIRM SUMMER CLERK'S EXPERIENCE
Midsummer Knight's Dream

If you have religiously followed our suggestions on interviewing technique, you should by now have received several offers from firms who want you to be their slave for the summer. But how to decide? This is a two-step process:

☐ IDENTIFYING THE PROPER FIRM: Separating the Blue Chip from the Buffalo Chip

There are two (2) categories of summer clerkships: (a) the Big Firm Clerkship; and (b) all others. This is not meant to "put down" a clerkship at a smaller, less prestigious, and most likely inferior firm. This is simply a convenient way of ignoring such positions.

"Other" clerkships are ignored because, frankly, they lead to jobs (at best) and anonymity (at worst). Thus, it is important to tag inferior firms early on if you are to avoid the stigma and intellectual opprobrium attached to their summer programs. Unfortunately there is no hard-and-fast method by which to identify such firms with 100% accuracy. There is, however, hope: through painstaking research, exhaustive canvassing, $50 in small bills to the author, and proper use of the following guidelines:

Does Your Prospective Firm

☐ Post job openings at the local employment office as well as at your law school?
☐ Offer to reimburse travel expenses for an on-site interview (but only up to the value of a bus transfer)?
☐ Insist that all attorneys wear a sport coat if they are expecting paying clients?
☐ Accept MasterCard or Visa as payment in full?
☐ Request that you submit to time trials in the 40- and 100- yard ambulance dash in addition to providing writing samples?
☐ Display "flexibility" over the issue of whether the writing sample was actually written by you?
☐ Advertise "fixed fees" in local

newspapers for simple wills, divorces, and antitrust suits?
☐ Boast of client stable that prominently features nicknames like "Mom," "The Waiter," "Knuckles," and "Blood Gutter"?

Any of these questions answered affirmatively should trip the warning switch in your mind and convince you to leave the interview immediately under *any* available pretext (e.g., the uncontrollable urge to rotate your car's tires, clean your room, check out the results of an AIDS test).

Conversely, there is no true litmus test you can employ to identify a "proper" firm with which you can summer. This is largely because hiring partners in veddy proper firms do not secrete enough saliva in the normal course of a 20 minute interview to enable you to use litmus paper. It is also because almost anybody can elbow his way into the yacht club these days. But once again, a few pointed questions combined with heads-up play will serve you well.

Does The Firm

☐ Acknowledge that its salaries are "competitive" and refer to Dave Kingman's salary as a "ballpark" figure?
☐ Offer challenging summer assignments like tracking down a marginal witness "somewhere off Champs Elysees," a task which they admonish you may well have to complete before the turn of the millennium?
☐ Agree to fly you out for a long weekend, but only if you agree to fly first-class to compensate for the inconvenience?

Affirmative responses to these and similar questions will indicate paydirt. Should you possess enough of the right (or nearly right) stuff to shake the man's hand at the end of the interview, you have now stepped onto the threshold of the best boondoggle since the Brooklyn Bridge was sold to a group of investors as a tax shelter (revenues from tolls just about equaling the monthly carrying charges).

☐ HANDLING YOURSELF WITH APLOMB

Of course, it's a dirty job and somebody has to do it. Somebody has to take a summer off for the purpose of saving IBM, rendering candid but helpful opinions to Citicorp, and merging Ford with GM over the objections of the Justice Department. It might as well be you, especially since you have retained at least a few notes from the small-group seminar in Law and the Void, which should enable you to skirt any intellectual problems arising from these delicate maneuvers. You have enough of the social graces to resist the urge to goose the senior partner's daughter in public. You are toilet-trained. So, the issue boils down to wardrobe. Will Lee Iaccoca embrace you when you meet this summer? Taste, among other criteria, will tell.

TASTE TEST

Brown shoes are worn with blue suits:

a) only in Brooklyn.
b) only in my dreams.
c) only in my worst dreams.
d) at every opportunity.
e) at every opportunity in Modesto.
f) (a) and (e).

Although (a) and (e) may well be correct, the *best* answer is (c), "only in my worst dreams." Those of you who cannot (or will not) dream in color may have been penalized here, but too bad. We have compiled a list of summerwear "no-no's" for each of you. Those of you with better things to do may elect to turn the list over to your valets for immediate action. The rest of you had better read on.

Dressing for failure is not easy. Yet, most law students have the knack. We have put together a few hints here, but the soundest advice seems to be: "Dress as if you were going directly from your office to the undertaker." Thus, you should avoid:

- ☐ rep ties which feature colors not found in nature, or which reflect light, or both;
- ☐ "club" patterns featuring Negro jockeys, coupling nymphets, sports logos, or airline insignias;
- ☐ Thom McCann footware of all shades and styles;
- ☐ short-sleeved shirts with built-in pocket protectors;
- ☐ Italian-cut anything.

☐ OFFICE POLITICS:
Anything Worth Doing Is Worth Doing avec Savoir Faire

Dressing correctly does not, of course, end the matter. Correct behavior also plays a role in your success. For example, you have been assigned to "expand upon" a memorandum written by a junior partner a month earlier. You discover that the case upon which he relies was not only overruled, but was stoned to death and dragged through used circus sawdust by the Supreme Court of the United States.

Do you
- ☐ point this sad fact out in a scathing memo directed to all members of the management committee?
- ☐ note the oversight in a letter to the client?
- ☐ send an anonymous photocopy of the death-dealing case to the junior partner?
- ☐ take him to lunch, point out the oversight, and offer him a pistol with one bullet in the chamber and urge him to do "the right thing"?
- ☐ do nothing at all?

Of course, the correct answer is to take the junior partner to lunch, offer him the gun, and expect him to do the right thing. If he goes through with it, you can be sure that you have landed the correct firm, and you can also be confident that you have handled yourself with the requisite good taste.

Most conflicts in summer programs do not arise in such stark situations, however. You should be prepared to mix it up with the best of them at the yacht club, sail into dangerous waters with senior partners on their boats, eat expensive lunches, and display a witty cocktail style. You should also keep that gun handy—you may need it, because the worst damage to your summer career is typically done by your fellow summer associates.

Other summer associates, like bad heroin in Watts, are just a fact of life with which you must deal. Most will laugh at your law school, demean the quality and quantity of your work, and generally do anything short of taking hostages to ensure that *they* get *their* offer of a permanent position. The gun ploy generally fails because they are ready to die if it will guarantee them an offer. And most are smart enough to avoid the "tasty" homemade brownies you might offer.

You are surrounded, it's as simple as that. In the words of Pogo Possum, "we have met the enemy, and they are us." Don't allow yourself to become paranoid, however; you have nothing to fear but your own (treacherous) comrades, who are impatiently waiting for you to expose a vital organ. But you will just have to weather them like a visit to a Contract Killers' convention. Fortunately, law school prepares you for such siege behavior. So just relax, behave normally, and keep your back to the wall at all times.

SECTION V
BREEZING THE BAR
Bambi meets Godzilla

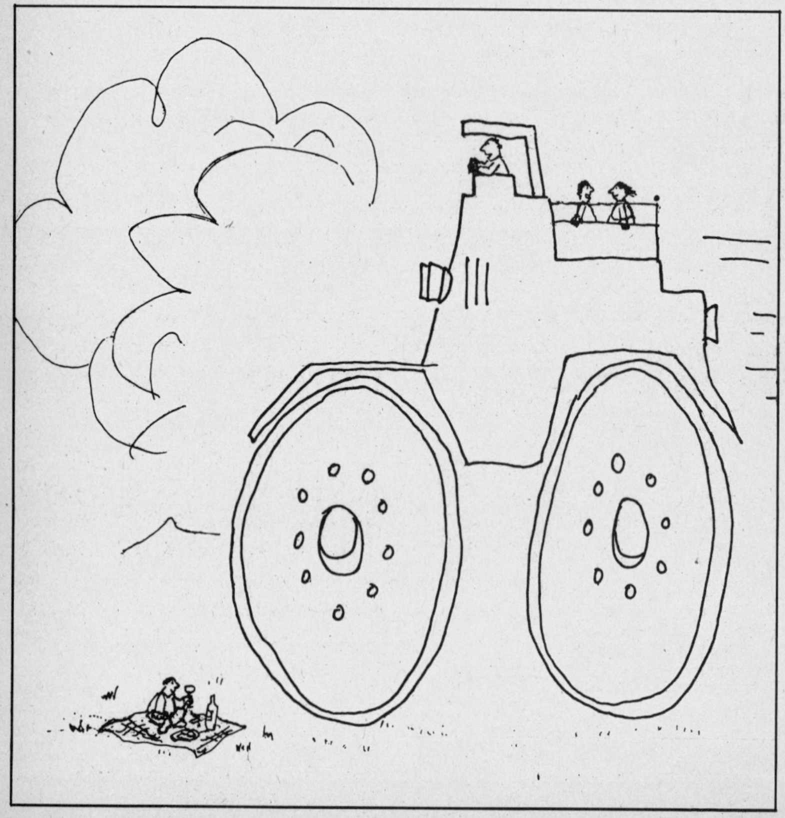

CHAPTER 15
BAR WARS
A Look at the Bar Examiner's Empire

An Inspirational Message from the Publishers

Congratulations! You've breezed through law school, aced law review, and been asked to join a prestigious law firm. It's all sewn up. Basically, the only thing you have left to do is sail past the Bar, and you're home free! Go get 'em, tiger!

Equal Opportunity Response from the Writer

If the above message has made you feel confident and put you at ease, terrific. You should be. A similar speech was given to the Marines just before they landed at Iwo Jima. ("All we have to do is breeze past the beaches, guys, then it's easy!") and it worked on them.

The inspirational pep talk form was originated in 19th-century India and owes a lot of its success to a famous colonel, now defunct, who assured his troops: "Look—for all practical purposes, we've already won the whole battle. Let's just cruise through this valley, and we're in Fat City!"* (He may have used slightly different wording, but he was unavailable for comment afterward, so we don't have a verbatim account.)

But let's not beat around the bush. Contemplating, studying for, and taking the Bar is the single most brutal, inhuman, and excruciating experience you will ever endure in your life, with the possible exception of being stranded on a tropical island with Rodney Dangerfield.

---

*See "The Charge of the Light Brigade," A. Tennyson.

THE SORROW AND THE PITY: A Historical Overview of The Bar Exam

The idea of the Bar Examination began in England around the turn of the century. Prior to this time, attorneys-to-be were tested by tying weights around their hands and feet then throwing them into wells. If they floated, they were admitted to the Bar. One year, at the 210th annual convention of Bar Examiners (held in Sussex, in the Tudor Room of Denny's), it was decided that this was an inefficient and outmoded system, and besides, too many of the applicants were surviving.

So they resolved then and there to develop an exam that would achieve their stated aims without getting them arrested. They also resolved to beat the check, which they promptly did. (They slipped out while Norman Rutherford Hughes made a scene about finding a hair in his burger. By the time he sprinted out they had the horses revved up and made a swift getaway.)

THE MODERN BAR

After many revisions and permutations (not to mention bribes and kickbacks), the modern Bar Exam emerged. The exam you will face is held twice a year, at the end of July and at the end of February. Not coincidentally, these are also the dates when the Aztecs practiced ritual human sacrifices.

ESSAYS

There are two parts to the exam: The essay portion will contain six one-hour essays per day and will be one or two days in length depending on the jurisdiction. The essays test your ability to read a four-page fact pattern that looks as if it were translated from Dostoevsky's hallucinogenic notes, deciphering the 17 parties, 20 issues of law, and 42 plausible conclusions, and then reducing the whole process to paper without using profanity.

MBE (Multidimensional Brain Emasculation)

This section of the Bar Exam contains 200 multiple choice questions. Typical directions will instruct: "All of these answers are wrong. Choose the second-to-the-most-wrong answer," or "Which of these answers, which are all correct, is the third from the *least* correct?"

What is being tested here, of course, is your ability to withstand 26 Gs of high-altitude winds without blacking out, bleeding from the ears, or losing bladder control.

THE BAR EXAMINATION: England, circa 1606 Enthusiastic applicants impatiently await their turn.

☐ YOUR ALTERNATIVES: None

Now, this is really going to irk you, but the fact remains that if you intend to practice law in a state populated by more than cows and cornfields, you're going to have to take a Bar Exam. It's as simple as that.

Recent grads are, despite their protestations, resigned to the inexorability of the Bar Exam. It's like riding subways in New York—sooner or later someone's going to spray-paint "Fast Eddie 102" on the back of your shirt. It's inevitable, just a matter of time. This realization spawns immediate reactions in the Bar Trekkie which psychologists have broken down into four stages:

Anger
"The Bar Exam is an artificially constructed barrier to keep new lawyers out and to keep old lawyers fat."

Denial
"No *way* am I going to pay $800 to take a damn Bar Review course!"

Bargainging
The Trekkie promises herself various rewards for grinding it out. In a typical example, one student vowed he would give himself the luxury of taking all 26 of his roommate's Marvin Hamlisch records and spinning each one of them off the World Trade Center after buffing them one by one with a floor sander. Another student promised himself a brand-new BMW after the Bar, which he successfully acquired. Unfortunately, he was soon apprehended when the real owner spotted him driving the car.

Acceptance
At this point, the Trekkie throws up his hands and accepts the awful truth that the Bar is simply a horrible but inescapable fact of life, much like people who put plastic covers on their couches or name their cat "Cat" or have friends named "Binky."

The next step is obvious—the Trekkie now calmly breaks the problem into the following components:

What do I do now? WHAT DO I DO NOW? WhadodIdoonow?

What in *hell* do I do now? WhaddinhelldooIdoonow? Waddawaddahoonoo?

At this point, it is time for us to take a look at Bar Review Courses.

CHAPTER 16
BAR TREK
Preparing to Boldly Go where No Man Has Gone Before (and Survive)

Attempting the Bar without taking a Bar Review course first is like sky-diving without a parachute. It's like attending a Black Sabbath concert without earplugs. It's like playing opposite Dick Butkus without a helmet. It's like interviewing at Cravath dressed in a leisure suit. Your chances of success can be summed up in this way: none, zero, zilch. Sure, someone will tell you in an offhand manner that he studied for the bar by reviewing his notes from law school two days before the exam. It would not be accurate to accuse this person of stretching the truth; it would not be fair. He is actually lying through his teeth.

Beware: Out of the desire to appear both incredibly intelligent and disarmingly blasé, lawyers who have finally passed the bar are dangerous sources of misinformation.

You haven't truly experienced revisionist history until you talk to a lawyer who has passed the bar. It's like talking to someone with amnesia. "The Bar? Oh, it wasn't too tough. I just sort of took the course, then took the bar and passed. Just lucky, I guess." Whether he's merely trying to impress you, or attempting to block the ordeal out of his memory, don't buy it. It's not true.

You *must* take a Bar Review course. The only legitimate questions are "Which course should I take?" and "How can I get a deal on the outrageous price they're charging?" which leads us to possibly the greatest pearl contained in this book!

☐ BECOME A BAR REVIEW REP AND SAVE $800

At different times of the year, you will notice that a cluster of students have set up a table, just like a bake sale, only the goodies they are selling are a Bar Review Course (usually BAR/BRI or BRC). They will be jovial, helpfully answering the self-serving questions of passersby (e.g., "I'm top of the class, Order of the Coif, and President of Law Review. Do you *really* think I need a review course?" "No, you need a proctologist.")

Why are these individuals smiling? Because when third year rolls around and everybody signs up for one of the two major review courses (as 99% of them will), shelling out $800 or so for the privilege, these reps are enjoying a free ride. By becoming a rep early on, not only are you guaranteed a free course, but usually you are allowed to use all of the facilities (outlines, taped lectures, etc.) during all three years of law school. Do we have to spell it out for you?

Now that you've decided to take a course for free, the next question is: which course should you take?

☐ CHOOSING A BAR REVIEW COURSE

Ultimately, you will take whichever course your friends are taking so that you can borrow their notes. But if you are a trendsetter, or if you don't have any friends, these considerations should influence your decision.

1. What is the reputation of the course for the jurisdictions in which you intend to practice? A national course that prepares students for Michigan and California may be worthless in Florida. And it is common knowledge that Texas Bar courses equip students only for practicing law in Texas and certain other undeveloped Third World areas.

2. What is included in the price? A lot of courses offer 25 mouthwatering surefire seminars on beating the Bar, and it is only after you have made your deposit that they inform you that 24 of these seminars are "advanced" (i.e., cost another $100). "Oh, you're planning on taking the MBE as well as the essay? Why didn't you *say* so, you silly willy? That will be $300 more, please."

3. How available are the tapes if I can't make a lecture? All the courses *have* tapes. But tracking them down can be like searching for the Loch Ness Monster. A sneering administrator will growl: "Evidence? We played that tape *last* week on Tuesday night, in the whitefish section of Mindy's Deli, and later in the lingerie section of J. C. Penney's—it was in the schedule. Where were you? It's gone now."

4. Does the course format make sense? The course should start around the beginning of June (for the July Bar right after you graduate), should be in English, and should cover the subjects that will be on the Bar. Beyond that, follow your personal preferences. Some courses rely on mnemonics, some employ lectures only, a few are based on hypotheticals, most use outlines, some use meditation, and one that we've heard of uses acupuncture treatment.

The Bar Review course may be based on a combination of the following features:

- Outlines
- Lectures
- Mnemonics
- Meditation
- Isolation tanks
- Electroshock treatment
- Forcible tattooing
- Tarot reading
- Simulated testing
- Cross-country bicycle trips
- Bake sales
- Mud wrestling
- Seances
- Paramilitary maneuvers
- Suicide hotline
- Visits to Chinatown restaurants
- Psychiatrists
- Primal screaming

A famous lecturer for one course uses rock 'n' roll analogies. (i.e., unilateral contract—an offer which asks for acceptance by *action*, not a return promise. Like when Jim Morrison of the Doors says, "Come on baby light my fire," he's not asking for a *promise* to light his fire, know what I mean?) Another course features striptease lecturing. The lecturers remove an article of clothing for each concept until all aspects of subject are uncovered, after which they are applauded and promptly arrested.

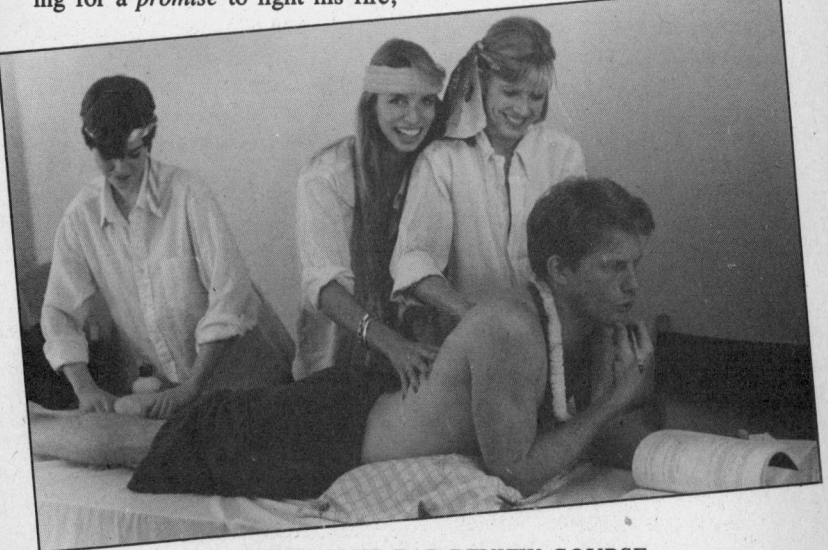

CHOOSING YOUR BAR REVIEW COURSE
Consideration #1: Does the course have the features I need to help me pass the bar? Studying for the bar is hard work. Here, Jon ponders a difficult Property concept while "features" Monique, Katrina, and Helga loosen those tense muscles.

CHAPTER 17
IN THE BELLY OF THE BEAST
A Personal (Horrifying) Account of the Exam

In spite of all of the speeches, lectures, and simulated tests you will get in your Bar Review Course, a nagging question remains: What does it *really* feel like to take the bar?

Unfortunately, this question must, of necessity, remain somewhat abstract unil that fateful moment, because taking the bar, like getting hit by a truck, must be experienced in person to appreciate its full effect.

However, in an effort to approximate the experience, we are reprinting in full the memoirs of Suzy Q, who was so compulsive about keeping an accurate journal that she filled out this entry while taking the exam. It is an intimate portrayal of one person's journey through that most grueling of rites of passage: the Bar.

☐ SUZY Q'S DIARY

ADVENTURES OF SUZY Q: BEFORE THE BAR

JULY 25

Dear Diary,
Last night I had the most amazing dream...
I'm sitting in row 3, seat 5. The room is deadly silent, except for two students screaming uncontrollably in row 6. The proctor, who resembles the executioner in "Country Club Kill-Fest," contemptuously tosses me my test with a cruel sneer. I keep the test but sell the cruel sneer to the schinocephalic hebbish sitting next to me for a cool $2.40. I tell the proctor to take off that black hood he's wearing, but he says it makes him look distinguished.

I leaf through the test and can detect no problems. This is because the test is written completely in Arabic. It could be a takeout menu for all I know; naturally I can't see any problems. The fat girl in row 2 who seems to be able to translate has just ordered two falafels and a baba ganoush from the street vendor outside. So it *is* a takeout menu.

And wouldn't you know it, my Bar Review course didn't cover takeout food at *all*, let alone Middle Eastern food, all of which seems to be a series of variations on deep-fried fur balls. For the first time, I feel the grip of panic around my throat. I desperately fight the grip, seeking its source. It turns out to be the redheaded guy behind me. I tell him to grip his own throat and give him a scowl, which he sells to the proctor for 35 cents. I get out my pocket translator-calculator and letter by letter, word by word, tortuously work through the first paragraph, which turns out to be the only one written entirely in English.

Oh my God! My calculator batteries have died—I should have used Duracell. I desperately glance at the clock. I can tell I have only 10 minutes left because Mickey's big hand is on the 5. I lean over the fat girl's shoulder, desperately trying to decipher her order. But she spots me and maliciously covers everything relevant with a thick blanket of tahini sauce. The proctor is shouting orders in a clipped German accent: "Ze test is *finish*! And you? Heh, heh, you *also* are finished." I am dragged kicking and screaming from the room and shipped off to a camp where normal, healthy people are turned into stereo salesmen for Crazy Eddie's....

I wake up in a sweat, thrashing restlessly from side to side. Thank God, daylight! It was only a dream—or was it? I look at my coffee table and there, to my horror, is a half-eaten falafel—with extra tahini!

JULY 26

Dear Diary,
Only 24 hours to go, and I'm a vision of serenity—if you disregard the fact that my hands are shaking so violently that I can't pour myself a cup of coffee.

▭ FURTHER ADVENTURES OF SUZY Q: THE BAR ▭

JULY 27

This is it. This is the day! I get out of bed. I feel strangely calm. Is it my two months of rigorous study that has made me feel confident about this morning? Or the 27 Valiums I took last night? Who knows—drugs are funny that way.

I hop into the shower. No, I'm definitely not nervous. I'm in control. Turn up the hot water, that's it. Calmly reach for the shampoo—wait a minute. I'm taking a shower with my clothes on. Okay, stay calm...don't panic. Everybody does it once in a while. Some very famous people have done this.

Dry off with hair dryer.

Dry off clothes with hair dryer. Damn, I *knew* I should have gotten the 1,400-watt model. Some maniac outside is honking his horn right under my window. Mustn't let it rattle me. Got to stay calm.

Go over list next to my bed. Dress, shower—ah, there's the problem—eat breakfast, pencils, pens, notes, lunch, clench guard (to protect my caps), elbow pads, lucky Spiderman mask, aspirin, Percodain...God *damn*. That car honking is driving me nuts. I can't concentrate.

I open the fridge. I try not to look at the zucchini surprise, which I made three weeks ago and which now resembles either a green shag-pile carpet, a science project, or a golf divot, I'm not sure which. Wait. Zucchini surprise. Of course! I heave it with deadly accuracy out the window, Tupperware and all. The car abruptly stops honking. I wolf down breakfast, checking my list: map to location—check; call cab—right, I did that last night. In fact he should have been here 10 minutes ago. I look out the window. *Hell*. My cab is covered with zucchini surprise.

Time to go. Gather up every item on list: 14 pens, 22 automatic pencils, lunch, clench guard, elbow pads, last-minute notes for cab. Notes for lunchbreak, notes for bathroom stall. Vague feeling I've forgotten something.

PRE-TEST

Arrive at test center. How ingenious. Who would have thought of holding a test inside a burned-out pier that has been deserted for seven years? There are 2,000 other students here huddled around 100 card tables. The "air conditioning" consists of two turbofans the size of swimming pools. It sounds like we're inside a 747 engine, or at a Ted Nugent concert.

The proctors are all escapees from a drug rehabilitation center. I don't mind the tattoos, but do they have to wear their riding leathers? They seem to have an equal facility with French, English, German, and Italian, which is to say they can't speak a word of any of those languages. What is this guy trying to tell me?

He is trying to tell me he wants to see my ticket. I confidently reach in my bag and—bingo, it's not there. I realize now that I put it where I was absolutely sure I would remember it, thereby guaranteeing that I'd lose it. I try to appear casual, but my hysterical crying gives me away.

The head proctor has agreed to let me take the test. Maybe he was sympathetic to my plight, maybe he was afraid of my switchblade. I don't know, and I don't care. I sit down at the table across from Ellen Kingston, Ann Edelstam, and Mike Semansky. To my left is Rich Ward, who is already practicing looking at my test booklet. To my right is Harvey Zavin, who is busy with the horserace section of the *Daily News*.

10 MINUTES TO GO

Laying out my pens and pencils, trying to clear my mind. I try to recall what I memorized last night, but all I can remember is the dirty words to "Louie Louie." Mike has finished methodically sharpening his 17 pencils and is now methodically sharpening the erasers.

Harvey is methodically figuring out the odds on the third race at Aqueduct.

Anne and Ellen are comparing schools, each trying to convince herself that she is better prepared. As it turns out, they both went to the same law school and were in the same class. And had the same miserable attendance record. This does not cheer either of them up.

QUESTION #1

I am given my test. This is it. The head proctor tests the microphone, which is turned up so loud it shatters two windows. The reverberations knock Rich's soda can off the table, and as if by instinct it spills directly on my lap.

The head proctor reads from his cue card in flawless third-grade broken English. He says something about "Do not open the test until I say so," but I am too busy reading the first question to hear him.

I dive eagerly into the facts of the first question, underlining, making notations, using the analysis I learned in the Bar Review course. What a relief! It looks like my training is paying off! I clearly recognize it as a Con law/Torts question. I immediately outline my issues, and then plunge into the answer.

I barely reach the issue of "standing to sue" when my sixth sense makes me stop writing. I double-check the facts, and discover, to my chagrin, that I have failed to make an obvious and critical observation. I was reading the instruction sheet.

Oh well, I think, maybe I'll get some credit for spotting the negligence issue. But I'll admit I am shaken.

Fortunately, the head proctor has not finished his speech yet. He is instructing students on the use of the life jackets located under our seats. I plunge into question #1. Richard, who has been copying my first answer word for word, crumples up his booklet with a look of disgust and hisses, "Get it together, man—this is serious business."

As I read question #1, underlining like mad, it becomes obvious that this is not a crossover question. It is a long and detailed question dealing

156 □ BREEZING THE BAR

with only one subject, rather than multiple subjects. The only problem is, which subject?

I narrow it down; it's either Torts or Con law or Trust and Estates.

Harvey's been writing nonstop. He seems pretty confident. I peek over at his outline. He has written his conclusion at the top, according to the instructions. I look at the bold scrawl. So that's it. Of course! Why didn't I think of it? "Lotsa Luck to win in the 3rd, with El Pendorcho to show." My admiration for his unequivocal conclusion is somewhat tempered by my desire to strangle him.

QUESTION #2

Finish first question, right on schedule. I hope to God it was a Crim Pro question. Look up. Ellen is still in the middle of writing her outline. She seems calm, but I can't help but notice that she is clenching her hands so hard her nails are turning purple and she has bitten through three clench guards already. Mike has finished sharpening his erasers and is now me-

Our spacious, elegant Test Center... très charmante.

thodically sharpening his pens. Richard irritably makes me move my hand, which I had inadvertently placed over my answer.

Skim question #2, underlining like mad. This is obviously a crossover question. It's either a Contracts/Secured Transactions/Property/Crimes question or its a Wills/Commercial Paper/Deep Sea Fishing/ Ballooning question, I conclude confidently.

I start my outline but it seems to be taking too long. Richard whispers in exasperation, "For Chrissake, forget the outline. We're falling behind!" He's right. Better just plunge in. The first paragraph goes smoothly; its only major flaw seems to be its total irrelevance. Richard rolls his eyes in disgust and starts copying from the guy to his right. I must admit I feel slighted.

QUESTION #3

Reading over this question I get a feeling almost like déjà vu, a feeling so familiar it seems like yesterday I confronted this question. Unfortunately the déjà vu feeling I am experiencing is complete nausea. I don't have a clue. I didn't yesterday, and I don't now.

The case seems to involve three circus bears, a French satellite, some overcooked ratatouille, a bus load of Hasidic Jews, two comical British detectives, a Mayan treasure map, the Nile River, and a poetry class at Sarah Lawrence. What the hell is this — a Bar Exam or a Tin Tin comic book? I concentrate on the Sarah Lawrence girls. They're the only ones who seem likely to sue, although you can never completely rule out a busload of Hasidic Jews.

What's that noise? Some guy's digital alarm watch has just started beeping. He tries to shrug it off, and laughs nervously, but the sound is drowned out by four students who, completely unhinged, are now beating him to a bloody pulp.

THE 10-MINUTE DRILL

I am in the middle of my concluding paragraph when suddenly a blast like a sonic boom, only louder, knocks the pen out of my hand. "YOUR ATTENTION PLEASE! YOU HAVE 10 MINUTES LEFT," roars the microphone. The wind created by the sound pressure blows the toupee off the head of a prematurely balding student sitting in front of the speakers. He goes completely crazy and runs toward the head proctor with every intention of throttling him. Fortunately, he can't reach his intended victim. This is because 15 other students are beating the proctor to a piece of meat loaf.

In spite of the pandemonium, I notice that Harvey has not only finished all three questions, he has handicapped 12 races. Mike, who has yet to begin the exam, is methodically sharpening his fingers; and Ellen, who has just started on the third question, is writing with both hands, one per page.

I am brought out of my reverie by Richard kicking me under the table. "Are you gonna finish your goddam test or not?" he demands impatiently. I plunge back in.

Just as I start my concluding sentence, another blast from the mike: "TIME IS UP! STOP WRITING! PUT DOWN YOUR PENS! CLOSE YOUR BOOKLETS! STOP WRITING!" All of this noise makes it tough to concentrate, but I bear down and continue writing. Just as I finish the sentence, I realize I have left out a major issue. I start a new paragraph with "While this issue is so self-evident it hardly merits mention..." and launch into the discussion. Richard gripes, "I wondered when you were going to get to that." Ellen is writing like mad. Mike has finished sharpening and is now reading the first question. Students are getting up. The assistant head proctor is shrieking, "STOP WRITING OR ELSE! PUT DOWN YOUR..." His voice stops abruptly when eight students beat him to a lump of liver pâté.

LUNCHTIME

I desperately have to go to the bathroom. I ask a proctor, who looks up from his knife game. "It's easy to find them. Go out of the pier room down the hall till you hit the elevator. Take the elevator down to the third floor, then go out the lobby, cross the street, and take a left. Go up the sidewalk about 50 yards—third bar to your right—"Cafe Central." Twenty minutes later, I can see Cafe Central." The line reminds me of when I bought tickets for a Stones concert.

All of the Bar Review courses stress that there is one absolute no-no during the Bar Exam. "*Never*, under any circumstances," they warn, "talk about the Bar with other students." To do so simply heightens tension and demoralizes the students involved so thoroughly that each goes back to face the second battery of questions with no self-confidence whatsoever, having become convinced during the course of the discussion with friends that he flunked the morning session.

So it is no surprise of course that *everybody*, bar none, is talking about the morning session. I speculate with Richard as to what will appear in the afternoon session. "I know *exactly* what we're going to get," he says confidently, "based on this morning's questions."

"Well, tell me," I urged. "Domestic Relations? Civil Procedure? Conflicts?"

"The questions we will get this afternoon," he announces sagely, biting into his ham-and-cheese sandwich, "will be ball-breakers."

AFTERNOON

Richard was right. I'm not going to talk about it.

Keen snapshot I took of a hapless student trying to take the only dignified way out---by strangling herself with her Pucci scarf.

JULY 30
MBE: THE SECOND DAY

Well, here we are again. Only this time it's the MBE. Just combine 200 *New York Times* Sunday crossword puzzles with the Heisenberg Uncertainty Principle and you've got the MBE. I see everybody's prepared. Rich has brought a special grading grid that he was "given" by the MBE administration because he was a "special case." He offers to share, but points out that it is keyed to his particular version of the test, so it might not help me unless I get the J-24 version too. My, he certainly seems to have found the inside track to this exam!

Anne and Ellen are chatting and exchanging recipes. I think Ellen's Sky-High Psilocybin Pie sounds pretty impressive, but I wonder how well the leftovers will keep. Mike has brought a special good-luck charm which he is wearing. Personally, I would imagine it gets pretty stuffy wearing a double-ply scuba wetsuit all day long on dry land, and I would think breathing through that snorkel for hours might get tiring, but if he thinks it will help, more power to him.

Harvey doesn't arrive. Instead, there is a new guy who introduces himself as Pat Hebenat. "Harvey couldn't make it today because he had to fly up to Belmont for a race. I'm sitting in for him," he informed me. It turns out that Pat is an experienced MBE "pinch-hitter" with an impressive 27-2 win-loss record. Mike immediately tries to sign him up, but it turns out Pat is booked for the next three years.

We get our tests. Richard finishes filling his answer sheet out before the proctor finishes his "Don't open your tests until I tell you" speech.

As I open mine, I try to remember what the MBE lecturer in the Bar Review course said. "Remember," he said, "the MBE is just a reading comprehension test. Read the questions and answers closely, and take the time to *comprehend* them, and the rest is easy." Reassured, I start to read the first question. Then all of a sudden it hits me. The MBE is a reading comprehension test. But so is Einstein's Theory of Relativity and Wittgenstein's Theory of Ontological Diversity. If you read them, and comprehend them, you're all set. But it is now occurring to me that *reading* something and *comprehending* it are two very different propositions, with the first proposition being the easier of the two by about 26 lengths.

For example, the question I am now reading (without comprehending) says, "Of the answers following the fact-pattern below, two are completely wrong. The other two are ludicrously wrong. One of them is actually a verbatim letter to the editor sent by a Mr. Wiedemann to *Dental Hygiene Weekly*. This is the least wrong answer. You are to pick the answer that is the opposite to the one to the left of the one which relies primarily on the second adjective in the answer which erroneously interprets the third most least right answer wrong. Or wrongly."

After some consideration, and two rereadings, I reach a conclusion:

Do not pass Go. Do not collect $200. Punt. Vamanose. Pull the rip cord. Resorting to Plan B, I blacken in a pattern based on the flag of Brazil, for which I get a lot of compliments from the group at my card table.

Mike has opted for a variation of the "blindfolded darts" technique. He holds his pencil over his head point down, then drops it point first onto his answer sheet, filling in the box closest to where the point hit. He is not shutting his eyes as required by regulation blindfolded darts rules, but his scuba mask is so fogged up that he has achieved the same effect.

Ellen is using the "hurt finger" system, spreading her fingers wide, then rapping them forcefully on the edge of the desk with a rapid downward slap. With this technique you then hold up your hand and feel which finger hurts the most. That is your answer.

She has switched to backhand because of the difficulty of the questions. In close calls, she is squeezing each finger just to be sure. I hear some screams. Some members of the group have started to crack.

One distraught student just discovered that he has been filling out a Scientology Personality Test ("I *thought* the questions seemed a little easy," he noted), and there are the regular bozos who have reached the last question with seven answer blanks left, or vice versa. The proctor is running around trying to arrange a swap in which the students who filled out too many blanks trade with the students who filled in too few.

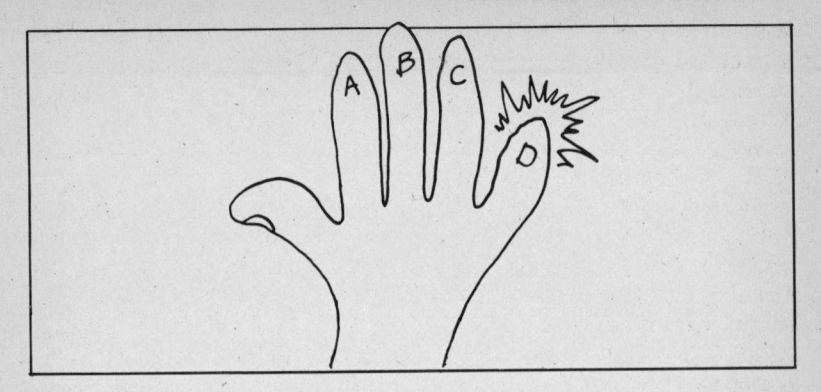

Pat, the mercenary, is taking the most systematic approach, eliminating two of the answers immediately using the big picture, then choosing between the remaining two by applying smaller considerations. Which is to say, he flips a quarter to narrow it down to two, then flips a dime to "home in" on the final choice.

Mike hasn't moved for 10 minutes. Rich is the first to notice, because Mike didn't pick up Rich's six of spades, and Rich knew he was keeping sixes. I wave my hand in front of his mask. No movement.

Then I notice his depth gauge. In horror, I realize the awful truth. His tanks ran out of air 15 minutes ago. Poor bastard. The Bar claims yet another helpless victim.

FOUR MONTHS LATER

I *passed*! Everybody at our *table* passed! Richard gave us the good news a week in advance. He said he "had access" to the scores and that "nobody will ever check," and so right he is! I frankly was amazed, since Anne had neglected to hand in her MBE test and I found to my surprise that I had taken my essay answers home by mistake. Horray! I am a big bad lawyer now! I don't have to keep forging names on pleadings anymore. Yahoo!

P.S. Mike is okay! He had just lapsed into a drug coma, which he snapped out of around Labor Day. He forgot the basic rule of "Methedrine before Phenobarb, except after Ether." Can you imagine how silly? Well, toodles!

CHAPTER 18
ADDING INSULT TO INJURY
How the Bar Examiners Decide Your Fate

Since preparing for and taking the Bar Examination is such a demanding ordeal, students are justifiably concerned that their efforts on the exam receive the kind of attention they deserve. Paranoia creeps up: "How *are* the exams graded, after all? How do I know that it's not a complete farce? Why is it that the passing percentage fluctuates according to local lawyer unemployment statistics? Why..."

To reassure you that you are not the first to suffer this angst, we are including highlights from a grievance letter written to the Bar Examination Committee by a group of young grads in 1958. In essence it charged:

1. The Bar Committee arbitrarily chooses the percentage that will pass, based on the economy for lawyers in that area during that year.
2. The Bar is skewed against minorities.
3. The Bar has no relation whatsoever to an individual's fitness to practice law.
4. It offers no system of appeal, since by the time you hear how the appeal went (and of course it will be denied), it is too late to study for the subsequent sitting.
5. The Bar is simply one more pointless, sadistic rite of passage in an inhumane system designed to imbue lawyers with a siege psychology which lasts throughout their careers.

Recently, the Bar Examination Committee addressed these grievances point by point in a position paper of their own which we have reprinted in full here:
1. What of it?
2. Too bad.
3. Who cares?
4. Tough.
5. So what are you going to do about it, pastrami breath?

Confronted by this seemingly callous response, attorneys-to-be from all parts of the country, fired with idealism against such an arbitrary and inequitable institution, have taken decisive action. United by common idealism, each struggled valiantly to pass the Bar, so that as full-fledged lawyers they could change the system for the better, thus preventing future students from having to suffer the kind of torture they themselves endured. Upon passing the Bar, each did pretty much what you would expect from bright young visionaries—they immediately began circulating petitions demanding that the requirements be tightened, and the essays be increased from 9 to 25.

So the institution of the Bar prevails, gaining strength daily. But back to the question "Will my exam get the individual attention it deserves?" The answer happily, is yes—each exam is handled personally by a qualified examiner (although "qualified" to do *what* remains unclear) for up to 17 seconds. We obtained the following exposé from an ex-examiner who managed to smuggle the information out before succumbing to Ibogaine poisoning.

☐ THE BAR EXAM: The Inside Story
HOW ARE THE QUESTIONS CREATED?

The same procedure is used in constructing questions for both the essay and the MBE sections. The Bar Examination Committee convenes at the house of the chairman, who is responsible for providing hors d'oeuvres and cocktails. Once everybody in the group is thoroughly plastered, they consult the source materials the research committee has accumulated throughout the previous year, which normally include common law cases of Lithuania, science fiction paperbacks, old Henny Youngman jokes, reruns of *The Twilight Zone*, Grimm's fairy tales, Zap Comix, the collected speeches of Henry "The Bloody Hammer" Kissinger, the *Reader's Digest* condensed version of *Finnegan's Wake*, *Penthouse* "Letters to the Editor," the uncut version of *Gone with the Wind*, and a full set of lawnmower instructions. Each committee member shouts out whatever pops into his or her head, and the secretary records every fourth word verbatim. The transcript is edited for pornography and then divided into either six or nine separate "questions," depending on the jurisdiction. The answers are derived by reversing the foregoing procedure.

GRADING THE BAR

To avoid arbitrary (and thus unequitable) results in grading the exam, the committee employs a rigorous two-step process.

Setting the Percentage
Prior to each sitting, the committee, employing various time-tested criteria, determines the exact percentage of students who will pass. The criteria include desirability of the jurisdiction, how many lawyers are already practicing there, the demand for new lawyers, salary levels of present lawyers, how much money these present lawyers have contrib-

HOW YOUR BAR EXAM IS GRADED: Setting the Percentage. Chief Bar Examiner W. C. "Bob" Belmont, showing good form, sets the passing percentage for the Summer 1984 exam: 46%.

uted to the Bar Examiners, and others.

To ensure fairness, the Examiners will keep the passing percentage of each summer's exam within 5% of the previous one. The winter exams traditionally have a lower pass rate. This is because the associates at big firms have already passed in the summer, so there is no pressure on the committee to pass the remaining students, who are usually public-spirited, minority, or foreign lawyers anyway.

ADDING INSULT TO INJURY □ 165

Individual Grading
The examiners assure skeptical students that their exams will be carefully graded. This is true; each exam is given individual attention. Again, there is a two-step process: First, the committee separates out all of the exams which have $100 bills taped inside the covers. These automatically pass. They then consult the lists provided by the major contributors to the Bar Examiners Retirement Fund and pass them.

The rest are graded on the "bell

curve." Each booklet is carefully thrown by an examiner at a 34-inch-diameter circle in the middle of the floor. As the booklets pile on top of each other, a small mound develops shaped exactly like a bell. The examiners then flunk the booklets starting at the far perimeter of the circle, working their way in until the predetermined percentage of failure is reached.

HOW YOUR BAR EXAM IS GRADED: Individual Grading. Dedicated Bar Exam graders work late into the night to insure that each exam receives personal attention.

AUTHORIZED PERSONNEL ONLY
BAR EXAM BEING GRADED!
Bar Exam Committee

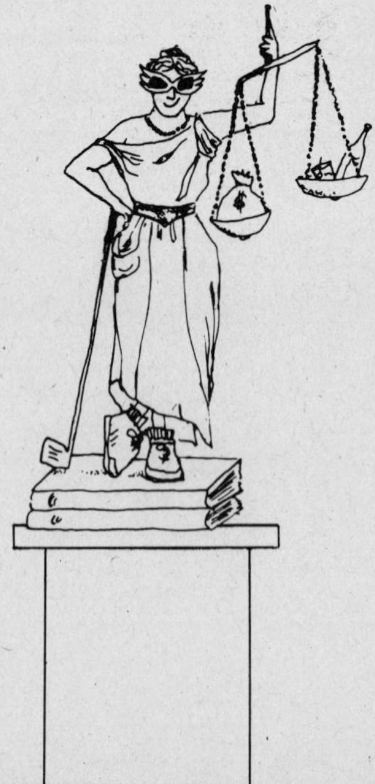

SECTION VI
"A" IS FOR ATTORNEY
Talking, Thinking, and Billing Like a Lawyer

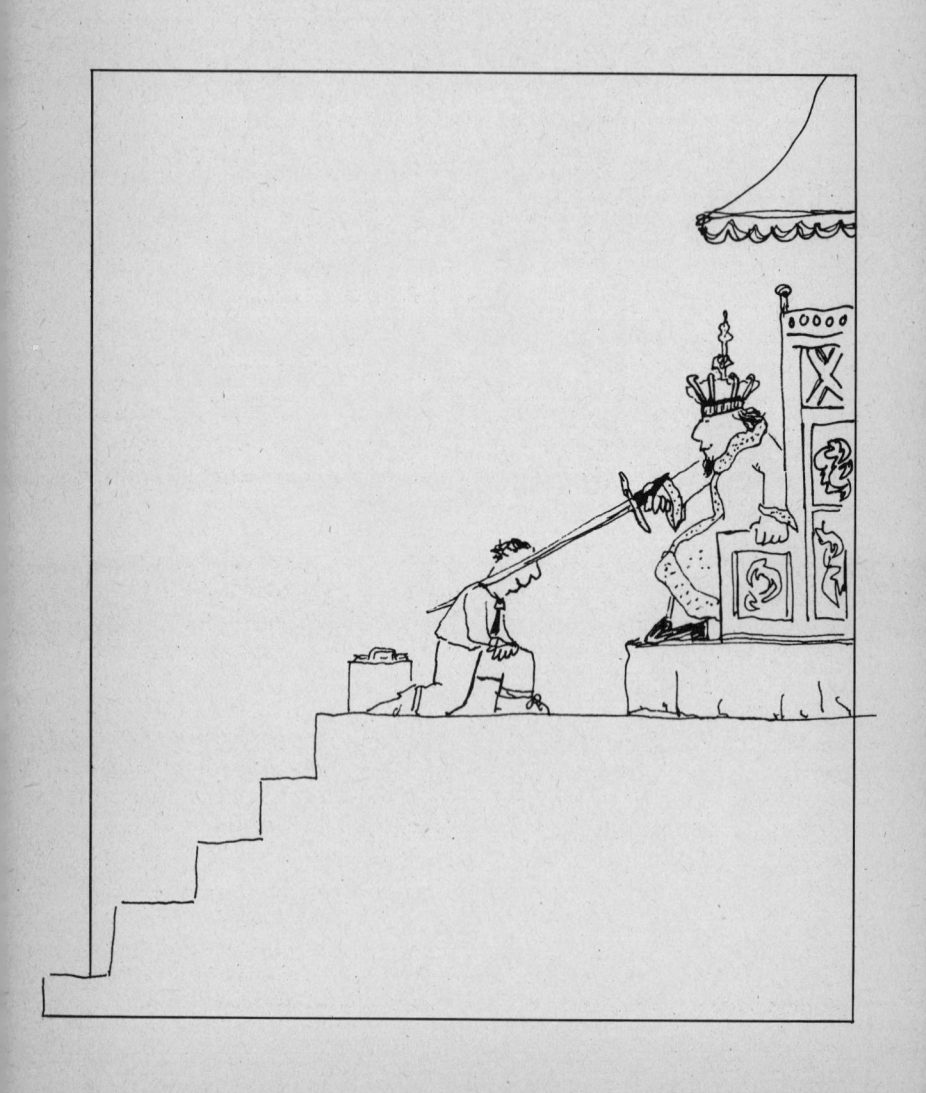

CHAPTER 19
LAW FIRMSMANSHIP
From Peon to Partner in Five Easy Pieces

So you've passed the Bar, and you're sitting in your tidy little associate's office (the one with the terrific worm's-eye view of the brickwork across the alley), wondering how to orchestrate your rise up the ladder from peon to partner. Muse no further, beleaguered one, because we have obtained, from the partnership committees of several major firms, an easy-to-follow Associates Almanac of Law Firm Behavior guaranteed to land you in a partner's office within three years.* The requirements are surprisingly simple. (Come to think of it, so are a lot of things if you look at them in a certain way. Take space travel: An astronaut has to (1) go up correctly, (2) come down correctly, and (3) not get hurt.) But they are critically important.

For easy comprehension, these requirements break down (as will you) into bite-sized pieces: practice peerless portage; work, work, work; buy Brooks Brothers; kowtow continuously and convincingly; eschew errors; bill boldly; and deploy power words at the slightest provocation. Here we go!

Let's say your job search has landed you in the litigation team of a Mega-firm. Almost immediately, if you are lucky, the partners will assign to you an indispensable role, one which will tax all of the skills you acquired on Law Review to the utmost. Just imagine—for the first two years of your associateship you will not only accompany partners into the courtroom, you will also have sole responsibility for what is universally recognized as the single most important element in big-firm litigation: porter service.

*Guarantee void where prohibited. Besides, we just said you would *land* in a partner's office—we didn't promise you would be allowed to stay there once the partner returned from lunch.

□ 171

☐ TOTE THAT BARGE: How to Carry a Partner's Briefcase

Your ingenuity and creativity in mastering this critical stage of big-firm litigation will be closely monitored to see if you are made of the right stuff for eventual promotion. As we said, this is where your law school experience—specifically, hauling around industrial quantities of *Federal Reporters*—will pay off.

The "Carry the Mountain to the Tiger" Zen Technique

The Turkish Twist

The Forklift

LAWFIRMSMANSHIP □ 173

TOTE THAT BARGE: Proven Techniques

□ MIDNIGHT EXPRESS: The Importance of Being Earnest

As any partner will be glad to remind you, God would not have put seven days in a week if he did not intend lawyers to bill for seven days a week. You have probably heard that on the seventh day, God rested. He could do this because he was running a sole proprietorship. You, unfortunately, are not allowed this luxury until you make partner. If you don't want to work seven days a week for the next eight years, join another profession (or successfully convince everyone that you're God).

Remember, there are workaholics who are not lawyers; but there are no lawyers who are not workaholics.

□ THE BROOKS BROTHERS MANIFESTO

Law firms existed for decades without the aid of synthetic fabrics. So can you. Most partners fondly yearn for the days before that ad campaign put the "yes" in pol*yes*ter. Don't be the one to remind them that times have changed. You may wear any button-down shirts you like, as long as they are white or pinstriped. Your three-piece suit may be any color you like, as long as it is blue or black. As for socks and suits, never mix argyle with black. Black socks look silly with an argyle suit. But then, *most* things look silly with an argyle suit.

☐ THE KOWTOW CATALOGUE

When in doubt, kowtow. Partners love a bright, aggressive, self-confident associate, provided he knows how to grovel like a mudguppy. Carefully orchestrated obsequious behavior can take the place of hours of hard work in advancing you up the legal ladder to partner. Practice your kowtow technique in front of a mirror by saying the following with a big smile:

"Why, *certainly*, Mr. Ropesend, I would love to babysit your three German shepherds for the next two weeks. They'll really give my studio apartment a homey feeling."

or: "Nonsense! I *enjoy* picking up your wife's dry cleaning. It's terrific excercise!"

or: "Of *course*! Do you want it watered two or three times a day! No problem! I'll just cancel my reservation. I hear the Caribbean is going to be rainy for the next two weeks, anyway. I'm glad you caught me before my flight was called."

"...I'm glad you caught me before my flight was called."

☐ MAKE NO MISTAKE ABOUT IT

To err is human—to forgive is not the partner's policy. Your approach to your work, from researching footnotes to chauffeuring the partner's son to his violin lesson, must be uncompromising. In a law firm, the saying "Anyone can make a mistake" is augmented with "... and get fired." The rationale is that you already made the single most inexcusable mistake of your life by becoming a lawyer. You will not be allowed another.

CHAPTER 20
POWER WORDS
A Glossary of Big-Firm Metaphors and Buzzwords for Heavy Hitters

Due to the rigorous selection process they practice, big firms are guaranteed a fairly uniform crop of red-hot young Turks and Turkettes each year.

These Turks and Turkettes will have all the necessary attributes in common:

1. Each has demonstrated an ability to fight his or her way to the top in law school.
2. Each has resisted the temptation to join the Ban-Lon revolution; their suits are not fire hazards, nor are they clad in fluorescent shades invisible to the human eye.
3. Each has expressed a willingness to say goodbye to life as he or she knows it (working 130 hours a week at law school) for life as the partner dictates it (working 168 hours a week at the firm), to give up bathing forever, to relinquish any remaining vestiges of self-respect, and most important to apply his or her nose, forehead, and entire facial area to the grindstone for six to eight years in the hopes of being made partner (a 37% chance in major New York firms).

At the end of those six years, a fortunate few will indeed be made partners, while the rest will be given their walking papers, forcing them either into solo practice or hara-kiri, two options indistinguishable to the big-firm senior associate. What is it—what is the ineffable quality that separates those who get the nod from those who get the ax? What separates the anointed from the dismembered? The blessed from the rest? All associates are indistinguishable in performance, appearance, and lack of social finesse. So what is the secret?

The answer, in a word, is two words: power words. Power words are tough metaphors, which are usually derived from sports, war, or safari hunting, and which, when properly used, lend a World War II panàche to any litigation.

Power words can elevate sewer litigation (where both sides shuffle boxloads of documents concerning, and full of, human waste products) to a titanic life-and-death struggle where John Wayne, Patton, and the boys in the band sally forth to battle against all odds to defend our homes, our cars and our families—in short, our whole way of life—while the forces of evil never sleep. Power words are essential to create the illusion that something cataclysmic (i.e., other than trading papers) is afoot.

Which is why the associate who can sling power words with the ease of an artillery master dumping salvos of 60mm shells on the enemy is partner material. He will be recognized first as a team player, then as a heavy hitter, and if he lasts long enough he may gracefully retire as an old warhorse.

The glossary below provides a starter's kit of power words for any situation. It is by no means exhaustive. In fact, the number of power words available is limited only by your imagination. Just take your metaphors from this context: Litigation is war. Or a gladiatorial contest. Or a professional sports game. It is *not* a spelling bee, remnant sale, or gin rummy game. Got it? Now prime your pump with these PWs, put on your helmet, and let's go after the big guns.

Play Hardball
A strategic decision, loosely translated as "Take no prisoners." Serving a summons on defendant as he is being wheeled in for triple-bypass surgery is playing hardball.

Take Off the Gloves
Essentially, "No more Mr. Nice Guy." A decision made somewhere around the fourth inning that we are now going to play hardball. Also, "Doing it by the book"—meaning no more informalities.

Thrill-Killing
Gratuitous violence just for the fun of it. Instead of merely impeaching a witness (which would be enough), demolishing him until he tries to take the only dignified way out—by strangling himself with his own necktie while on the stand.

Throw a High, Hard One
This term refers to a tactical move rather than a strategic decision. It is playing hardball, with a nasty surprise attached to the ball, in the sixth inning. Moving for a TRO at 4:00 p.m. on Christmas Eve is throwing a high, hard one.

Put on the Helmet (and Make Like Patton)
This antitrust case is going to take eight years, but if you keep us in gas, we'll fight till we make Moscow. This is the plaintiff's equivalent of "digging in for a long winter."

Mega-Firms
These are to normal law firms what the *Bismark* was to PT boats. Loaded with heavy artillery, capable of tak-

ing innumerable direct torpedo hits, stuffed with heavy-pack laborers, captained by old warhorses. Sinkable, but at what price?

Team Player
Someone who understands the concept of "strength in numbers" and the virtues of committee decision, and will not attempt to hot-dog it on his own. To be a team player is to be on the track to partner. There are two types of team players to avoid, however; players who have bad "raps":

The *"C" (Commitment) Rap team player*, unlike his cohorts, has the liability of a wife and family or mother in the hospital whom he insists on visiting for a few hours on weekends. This indefensible loss in billable hours takes him out of the running.

The *"J" (Judgment) Rap team player* is a hard worker, a great clone, but suffers from lapses in judgment when put in human situations. Of the eight-attorney team sitting in the courtroom, he is the one who wolf-whistles when the woman judge takes the bench.

Kamikaze
An attorney whose accelerator is locked to the floor, with no brakes or steering wheel. An all-or-nothing attack. Someone who turns down a $15.9 million personal injury settlement offer because he thinks he can get $16 million with a "good San Francisco jury."

Sleazebag
Derisive big-firm term for solo practitioner who works out of a phone booth. Also "Court Street lawyer"—an attorney who works the sidewalk outside the courthouse accosting pro-se plaintiffs for contingency fee arrangments.

(Going for a) Quick Kill
Fast motion for summary judgment; going for a KO in the first round.

Slow Death (The Long, Dark Tunnel)
Taking the long route, gradually bludgeoning the opposition into submission over an interminable period of time. A favorite of big firms, who inevitably win the war of attrition (they have *generations* of lawyers working on a case) by holding out until the original plaintiffs, and their descendants, have died off.

The Yellow Hammer
The final crushing blow. It is what waits at the end of the long dark tunnel.

Team Captain, Key Player
The team quarterback. If he's healthy, the team wins. If he's out with a sprained ankle, the team loses. Which is why his compensation contract has about three more zeroes on it than the other players'.

Heavy Hitter
A lawyer who hits for average. A gunner, well respected and feared in the business. An individual whose

client list includes more than five Fortune 500 companies. A heavy hitter is the rainmaker at a big firm.

Rainmaker
A lawyer whose particular reputation and style of rain-dancing results in a downpour of clients eager to lighten their wallets. Not necessarily a heavy hitter, but probably.

Long-Ball Hitter
Someone who gets the specific job done. Really done. If it's two outs in the ninth, bases loaded, and you need four runs, he will hit the grand-slam home run. Every time.

Warhorse
The Don. A former heavy hitter who earned his reputation the hard way, fighting (and winning) more gang wars than ten other partners combined. He now seems content to limit his "offers they can't refuse" to golf invitations, but remember: Old warhorses don't die—they're just put out to pasture. Beware when one comes out of retirement to "assist" your opponent in a case you are litigating.

Hod Carriers
Also "heavy pack laborers," "coolies," "bodies," "grunts," "scuttmonkeys." Any first-, second-, or third-year associates assigned to an antitrust case. The above synonyms reflect the generally high esteem you will command upon entering a firm at the bottom of the ladder. Associates are expected to lift that barge

and tote that bale until they die, and not ask questions or whimper.

Heavy Artillery

The big guns. Once you have decided to play hardball, and you're up against a heavy hitter, it's time to hit them with the heavy-bores: your own long-ball hitter, a squadron of battle-ready grunts, outside experts, discovery practice that relies heavily on C-130s—in short, a war with all the stops pulled out.

Sandbagging
Pointlessly stretching out battle on a matter completely unrelated to the merits of the case, focusing the opposition's attention on an irrelevant point with the intention of blindsiding them later. Cranking up thousands of billable hours on a maneuver designed solely to vex, annoy, and harass the opposition. The quintessence of a legal nonsequitur.

BRINGING IN THE HEAVY ARTILLERY: A long-ball hitter being borne to the courtroom by heavy-pack grunts driven by key player—the gloves are off.

Smokescreen
The defensive equivalent of sandbagging. Focusing on an outstanding parking ticket in a merger battle, then sending 3,000 interrogatories designed to "clear up the parking ticket matter." Creating an (irrelevant) trial within a trial.

Blind-Siding
Approaching someone from his "blind spot" while he is unaware (usually because he is concentrating on your sandbag diversion), then turning him into Hamburger Helper with the big guns before he has a chance to react. Norman asks Donna if he can have an extention of time on the deposition date she has called as he is on the verge of a breakdown and has planned a two-week vacation. She agrees graciously, then files an ex-parte TRO as soon as he takes off for the vacation.

Putting Them Through Hoops
Leading the opposition through every twirl in the "Discovery Dance." Hitting all crosscourts; making them run to one side, then the other, then back again, then a drop shot, then a lob. And all of this is before you hit them with industrial quantities of interrogatories, summons, and requests for admissions.

Smoke 'em Out
In a subtle attempt to elicit damaging admissions, a big firm will occasionally insert questions in discovery which are *not* solely de-

signed to vex, annoy, and harass. When the other side is dug in deep, you send in flamethrowers to find out where they are hiding their cache. These cleverly disguised "mines" are just waiting for an unwitting associate drone, exhausted after 15 hours of answering pointless questions (smoke-fatigue), to slip up and step on one, thus making a crucial admission.

Document Dump
Also called "backing up the boxcar," "snowing them under," "data dump," "unloading the avalanche." This is the defensive equivalent of "putting them through the hoops."

Its name derives from an exchange between a solo practitioner plaintiff and a Mega-firm defendant.

SOLO P: Have you sent over the documents and answers to interrogatories I requested?
MEGA F: Sure. Where do you want us to pull up the boxcars?

Say you would like to know the salary of several of the phoneworkers of AT&T. Mega F obliges, by sending you every pay slip of every employee of AT&T national and international for the last 10 years. The evidence is currently being housed in 15 high school gymnasiums.

THE DOCU-DUMP

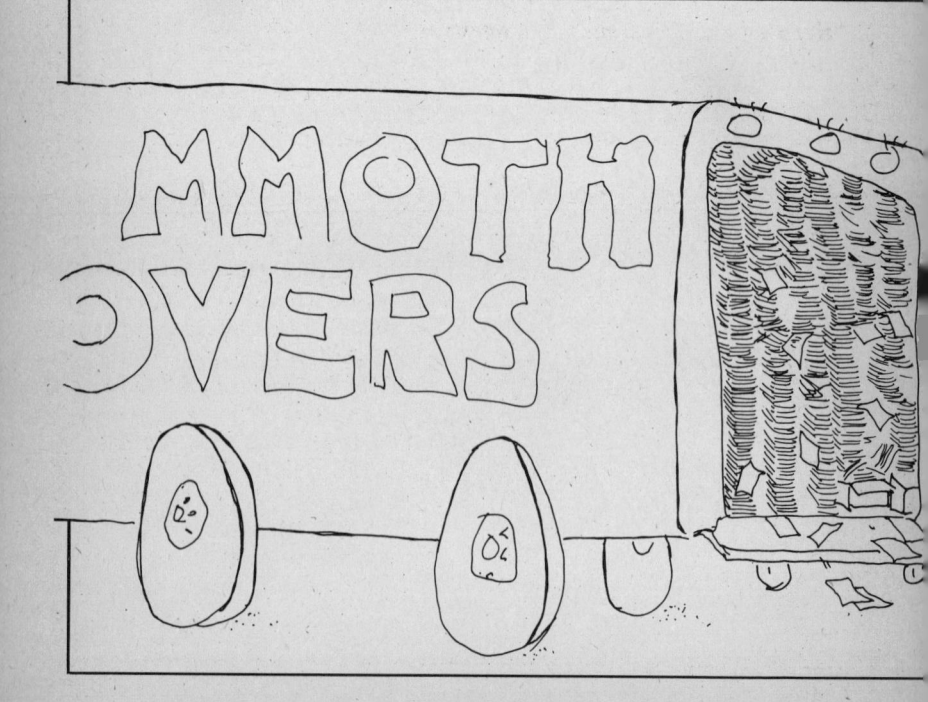

A well-orchestrated document dump can keep 30 grunts busy for 10,000 man-hours looking for the needle in an Everest-sized haystack. Once, seven associates were buried under an unexpected interrogatory avalanche and it took rescue workers two weeks to dig them out. Needless to say, frostbite, lack of oxygen, and paper cuts had taken a tragic toll.

Tag-Team
Also called "island hopping." Used against a solo practitioner. Depositions are scheduled Monday in San Diego, Tuesday in Chicago, Wednesday in Miami, Thursday in Reno, Friday in New York. Each of the five Mega-firm associates assigned to the case is resting up in a first-class hotel in his chosen city, waiting for the depo. We don't have to tell you what the solo practitioner is doing.

Torpedoes
Taking a few direct hits. Running into a few ugly surprises. For example, your star expert witness blurts out in deposition that he is the secret lover of your client. Proper phrasing when describing the setback would be: "Well, we took a couple of tor-

"Here are the documents you requested, sir."

pedoes in that deposition." Or: "Remember these points we were relying on? Well, forget them."

Take a Bad Hop
When your prize witness, although well primed and confident, has an inexplicable lapse into candor and truth on direct. For example, instead of saying, "I was bowling with the boys," he says "I was visiting the plaintiff's house with a gun." Such surprise bounces can be fielded by an expert, but they're annoying just the same.

Soft-Pedal
Also called the "What smoking pistol?" or "What elephant?" defense, a soft-pedal is an attempt to depict the St. Valentine's Day Massacre as "just a few of the boys having fun." If the opposition insists on bearing down, the soft-pedal matures into the "Look, let's be reasonable" stage. When the plaintiff's counsel offers as Exhibit A not only the smoking gun, but a high-speed photomontage of the bullet leaving the chamber and striking its client, it's time to be reasonable.

Probate Knuckler
I am the beneficiary, the witness, and the executor, and I intend to deal with myself at arm's length. Honest!

FYIGMO
Means "F *** you, I've got my orders."

When a six-year associate discovers to his chagrin that he will never be asked to join the inner circle (in effect, "given his orders"), he does not leave the firm in a huff. He simply puts it in Park 'n' Lock, and coasts. He doesn't involve himself needlessly (or otherwise) in any of the firm's activities; rather, he spends his time taking long lunches, wooing prospective clients to his new firm, and collecting his paycheck. His answer to anyone who feels that he should continue to plunge in enthusiastically "for the well-being of the team," rather than glide, is—you guessed it—"FYIGMO."

CHAPTER 21
LEGAL THINK
State of Innocence v. State of Siege

☐ DO YOU THINK LIKE A LAWYER NOW?

Whether you are aware of it or not, an ineluctable change has come over you during your three years of law school as a result of the endless case-briefings, all-night study sessions, Socratic sparring, and constant inundation in the adversarial system of inquiry. There are telltale external signs although you may not have noticed them. For example, you will *never* again answer a question (especially an "emotionally laden" one) with just the word "yes" or "no." When you see a plane crash on TV you will *never* again say, "Oh, those *poor* people and their families," and end your train of thought right there. The phrases you will use most frequently in your active vocabulary will be "define your terms," "it depends," and "on the other hand."

But there are more subtle and profound changes than these that indicate that you have traveled the path and achieved enlightenment. Your performance on the following Legalthink Test will let you know whether you have scaled the tower of babble, achieved Nirvana, and are ready to join the lofty ranks of Donald Segretti, John Mitchell, and Richard Nixon (a former president). Simply read the question, assess it, and act on your first impulse.*

1. An all-out nuclear holocaust that destroys every living thing on the planet is not a good idea.
    a) true
    b) false
    c) insufficient facts to make decision

2. You are playing rugby and an opposing player hits you below the belt. You
    a) bite him on the ear.
    b) kick him in the shins.

*Editor's note: If the reader's first impulse is to force-feed this book to his garbage disposal, or to set his sofa on fire, we are not liable for the damages.

c) threaten to sue his ass off after the game.

3. An 89-year-old widow, blind and crippled, was evicted from her apartment in the middle of December. She caught pneumonia and died. Which is closer to your reaction?
   a) The landlord's action is indefensible. That is the most disgraceful, sad, disgusting thing I ever heard.
   b) When was the last time she paid her rent? And did she have a preexisting medical condition?

4. Can we ever presume to measure the value of human life?
   a) Of course not.
   b) Sure. Approximately $867,000.

5. $2+2=4$
   a) true
   b) false
   c) It depends.

6. You are shipwrecked. A shark grabs your raft in his jaws and tows you 20 miles to shore. You regard this as:
   a) a miracle.
   b) professional courtesy.

7. Bribery and extortion are
   a) reprehensible and immoral.
   b) nice work if you can get it.
   c) nowhere near as effective as creative billing.

8. The movie that most accurately depicts the role of lawyers is
   a) To Kill a Mockingbird
   b) Mr. Smith goes to Washington.
   c) The Seven Samurai.

9. A man will never be convicted in a just society as long as he
   a) obeys the laws of god and man.
   b) retains a 200-attorney firm.

ANSWERS

First of all, if you are a proper lawyer now, you would not have read a single question before determining whom to bill for your time. Presuming that you launched into the quiz pell-mell under the assumption that the accounting department would "round up the usual suspects" and bill one of them, we come to the second true test of lawyerhood. You were told to "act on impulse" in answering each question, which means, of course, that you should follow your instincts and shoot from the hip—*after* devoting no less than three hours per question assessing all of the possible legal ramifications.

If you spent less time than three hours pondering each question, you are not only too reckless to be a first-rate lawyer, but you have no concept of billable time. You are probably the type who, when a partner asks you to "dash off a quick rough draft" of a brief for a case he is litigating, will give him something other than a polished, court-ready document. Perhaps you should consider some other profession better suited to your impetuous nature, like joining a motorcycle gang, or becoming a criminal lawyer.

Now, as for the answers: If you did not choose the *last* answer in each case, you have wasted your tuition. Go back to taking bad photographs of sailboats. However, if you unerringly gravitated (after the requisite three-hour contemplation) to the right answer in each case, welcome to the fold! You are a lawyer, you think like a lawyer, and you walk, talk, and act like a lawyer (despite repeated requests from the Board of Mental Hygiene). The world is your truffle.

You have the power to save the world, but if you play your cards right, you can avoid that onerous task. Your role hasn't changed since biblical times, when a confident client enthused, "Yea, though I walk through the valley of the Shadow of Death, I shall fear no evil—for I have retained the meanest SOBs in the valley."

The message is clear. And still pertinent. A modern-day legal expert recently assessed the lawyer's place in modern society with this upbeat analysis: "When the going gets vicious, the vicious turn pro." He then quickly added, "...and make lots of money." And who are we to argue?

Well, partner, here is where our paths diverge in our odyssey from here to attorney. It's time to bid a tearful farewell and get on with the work that has to be done. If you found any of our hard-won advice instructive, helpful, or just plain amusing, we've accomplished our goal.

You'll be receiving an itemized bill in about two weeks.

ABOUT THE AUTHOR

Kevin P. Ward, Esq., was educated at Harvard, an institution that transforms spoiled, irresponsible children into spoiled, irresponsible adults, and Hastings Law School, which turns them back again.

He currently resides in New York, a city that boasts more lawyers than pigeons.

℗

More Humor Books from PLUME

(0452)

☐ **THE OFFICIAL M.D. HANDBOOK by Anna Eva Ricks, M.D.** The life of a doctor—from med school to malpractice insurance. A humorous account of doctors and their world. (254388—$4.95)

☐ **THE OFFICIAL J.A.P. HANDBOOK by Anna Sequoia née Schneider.** This complete guide to Jewish American Princesses and Princes is an inside look at everything—from well-known traditions to long-kept secrets—that makes a JAP a JAP. (253594—$5.95)

☐ **THE BUTCH MANUAL by Clark Henley.** Throw out the heels and get out the construction boots. There's a whole new drag and it's called butch. No one is born butch, but with this instructive handbook, you too can be butch. (255493—$5.95)

☐ **NO BAD MEN: TRAINING MEN THE LOVEHOUSE WAY by Dr. Barbara Lovehouse as told to Anne Sequoia and Sarah Gallick.** Now, "the supreme male trainer of the universe" shows you how to train *any* man—without using a choke chain! Learn how to make your man's "tail" stand up straight; how to stop a man from straying; how to feed and care for your man; how to make him fetch such items as fur coats, engagement rings, flowers; and much, much more. (255023—$4.95)

All prices higher in Canada.

Buy them at your local bookstore or use this convenient coupon for ordering.

NEW AMERICAN LIBRARY
P.O. Box 999, Bergenfield, New Jersey 07621

Please send me the PLUME BOOKS I have checked above. I am enclosing $_____(please add $1.50 to this order to cover postage and handling). Send check or money order—no cash or C.O.D.'s. Prices and numbers are subject to change without notice.

Name_____

Address_____

City_____State_____Zip Code_____

Allow 4-6 weeks for delivery
This offer subject to withdrawal without notice.